BLUE HEAVEN

BLUE HEAVEN
Manchester City's Greatest Games

IAN PENNEY

Foreword by Fred Eyre

MAINSTREAM
PUBLISHING

EDINBURGH AND LONDON

The moral right of the author has been asserted

First published in Great Britain in 1996 by
MAINSTREAM PUBLISHING COMPANY (EDINBURGH) LTD
7 Albany Street
Edinburgh EH1 3UG

ISBN 1 85158 872 8

A catalogue record for this book is available from the British Library

Typeset in Garamond
Printed and bound in Great Britain by Butler and Tanner Ltd, Frome

To my wife Sheila, for putting up with me, my hobby, my mess (I call it research), my late nights, my vanishing acts and 'That bloody book'.

ACKNOWLEDGEMENTS

Acknowledgements to John Maddocks for help with the match reports, his 'On the Bench' recollections and the continuous 'can you check this?' phone calls, Phil Noble for the programme and ticket illustrations, Joanne Parker and the *Manchester Evening News* for once again supplying me with all the photographs, Fred Eyre for his generous and entertaining foreword, Mike Summerbee for the use of the club crest and his usual support, John Buckley for many hours with the microfilm viewers at Manchester Central Library and his wife Carol in the photocopying shop, and the 'On the Bench' contributors: James H. Reeve, Nick Conway, Stan Gibson, Gary James, Vince Miller and John Stapleton. And finally the 12 City players whose stories and anecdotes make up the pages of this book. Without their help none of it would have been possible and I would like to take this opportunity to declare my appreciation of their generosity towards me.

Ian Penney
June 1996

Contents

FOREWORD

I panicked a little bit when I was asked to write the foreword to this book, and any long time City supporter knows the meaning of the word 'panic' – that's when you are standing behind the goals at 'The Scoreboard End', holding your breath because City are winning one-nil with a minute to go and Dave Ewing has got the ball at his feet, in his own six-yard box facing Bert Trautmann . . . believe me, that is panic! But I was worried I thought I might be asked to write about a memorable City game that I had actually taken part in. To make Manchester City reserves versus Stoke City reserves sound like an epic encounter would be expecting a little too much even from me. Memorable games for the club, though, that is a different story and quite easy for me because I have been lucky enough to have seen City play in the '40s with Big Frank Swift, the '50s with 'The Revie Plan' and Lee, Bell and Summerbee in the '60s. The '70s brought a League Cup final win, another FA Cup final appearance in the '80s and Premiership football in the '90s. I've seen them all!

However, you never forget your first game. For me that was the last home fixture of the 1948–49 season – Manchester City 0 Arsenal 3 – not much changes! I was one of the 27,955 who watched 'Swifty' pick the ball out of the net three times, but didn't experience the joy of seeing any fly past the Arsenal keeper at the other end. Bert Sproston and Eric Westwood were the two full-backs, Sproston wearing a knee bandage 'to stop his leg falling off' as I was told when I asked what it was for. Bill Walsh, Joe Fagan and Albert Emptage made up the half-back line, with Hogan, Andy Black, Jones, Linacre and Roy Clarke in attack. I did not see any goals for City that day, but my young eyes had seen enough for me to know that I wanted to be a footballer when I grew up – and that there was only one team I wanted to play for. Of course there have been many memorable games since then, but apart from the obvious cup finals, semi-finals and European games, for sheer nail-biting, white-knuckle tension, the last game of the 1958–59 season – at home to Leicester City – is the one that I remember as the best.

Wednesday night, 29 April. Portsmouth were already relegated – City had to win to avoid going down with them – whilst Aston Villa who had come to Maine Road the previous Saturday and pinched a nil-nil draw were in the same position: they had to beat West Bromwich Albion at The Hawthorns to stay in the First Division.

As you would expect, the City lads made us suffer just that little bit more by going a goal down after just nine minutes, before Joe Hayes headed home a Bobby Johnstone cross to make it 1–1 at half-time. Just after the break Johnstone sent Ray Sambrook away to send us into raptures for the second and Billy McAdams bravely hustled in the third. . . but that wasn't the end of the drama! The West Brom–Villa game had kicked off 15 minutes earlier and the score from the Midlands was hoisted up on the old scoreboard behind us every quarter of an hour. With two minutes to go Villa were winning 1–0 and if things stayed as they were at both grounds, then City would be relegated on goal average. A grim prospect indeed.

It was then that fate – in the shape of West Brom's England centre-forward Ronnie Allen – took a hand as he fired in Albion's last-gasp equaliser. This goal kept Manchester City in the top flight, and at the same time consigned Aston Villa – and ironically their manager Joe Mercer – to a season in the Second Division. Manchester City's team that electric night was: Bert Trautmann in goal; Bill Leivers and Ken Branagan the full-backs; Roy Cheetham, John McTavish and Ken Barnes the half-backs; and Colin Barlow, Bobby Johnstone, Billy McAdams, Joe Hayes and Ray Sambrook in attack.

Six months after that marvellous evening I signed for the club as a groundstaff boy, and found myself training and playing every day with all of those players – with the exception of Bobby Johnstone who had moved back to Hibernian. That really is the magic of football. . . and of Manchester City.

Enjoy this book, it really will bring back some happy memories.

Fred Eyre

INTRODUCTION

In the autumn of 1994 I was invited to Maine Road for the launch party of *The Battle For Manchester City*, a new book by the highly respected *Daily Mirror* sportswriter Alec Johnson. The book was published by the Edinburgh-based company Mainstream – a publishing house who were at the time 'doing a Martin Peters' in the sports publishing world. By this I mean they were 'sneaking in on the blind side', by producing books of both high quality and great commercial value. Over the following two years I believe they have built steadily on this reputation and are now surely the number one publishers of sports books in the United Kingdom. No mean feat when you look at some of the other players in the field – many I'm sure with a lot more financial clout than Mainstream. (Nothing like a bit of grovelling to your publishers, is there?)

Anyway, back to autumn 1994. At that party I met Bill Campbell, a director of Mainstream, and the discussion centred around the imbalance of Manchester-based football books. I complimented Bill on his obvious good taste in publishing Alec's book and mentioned a couple of ideas I'd had (which by the way had been turned down by other publishers) for a City annual aimed primarily at the terrific Junior Blues following. Mainstream are not producers of 'annuals' as such, and so Bill politely turned down my ideas. (I was getting quite used to this by now.)

However, as the saying goes, every cloud has a silver lining. Within minutes of his rebuttal, Bill was offering me the opportunity to compile *The Maine Road Encyclopedia* for him. This was to be the latest in a well-established series which, if memory serves, already took in half a dozen or so other clubs. After I had picked myself up off the floor, I shook his hand and accepted his offer. So began a seven-month project involving newspaper cuttings, match programmes, interviews, reference books and the like. To say I enjoyed it is one thing – to say it was hard work is another.

The book came out in October 1995, and at the remarkable price of just £7.99, sold steadily almost from day one. Admittedly, not well enough for me to take possession of my own Caribbean island, but who wants to be Jeffrey Archer – apart from Jeffrey Archer, that is!

By all accounts the book was well received and was still being reviewed some six months after its initial publication. However, there was one very black side to all this. Almost as soon as the book hit the shelves it was out of date. The Blues suffered their worst-ever start to a season, players (including long-serving crowd favourites) went, new ones came, and worst of all, the dreaded 'relegation' entry would shortly need to be completely rewritten. Such is the nature of sports book publishing, with events changing literally every day.

Whatever happens at Maine Road, the one underlying factor in anything to do with Manchester City Football Club is the loyalty and passion of its supporters.

I have looked up the word 'rollercoaster' in the English dictionaries published by the UK's top three dictionary publishers, namely Harper Collins, Oxford University Press and Chambers. To my surprise none of them gives any reference to Manchester City, yet I cannot think of a single word more synonymous with our great club. As Fred Eyre suggests in his foreword to this book, you only have to see City once to know there will never be another club for you.

Just after Christmas 1995 I again met Bill Campbell, who asked me if I had any ideas for another book on City. Obviously paying no heed to the Blues' lowly league standing, he was apparently quite pleased with the success of *The Maine Road Encyclopedia*. I told him that I'd been toying with the idea of interviewing former players and getting them to describe in their own words one memorable game from their Maine Road careers. Bill liked the idea immediately and a formula for the book was established shortly afterwards. (Before anyone asks, no, I am still no nearer to that elusive Caribbean island.)

He liked the idea so much that he returned to Edinburgh and began to sign up authors to do the same project on other clubs. The players should be from different eras, thereby giving the book a wider appeal to the prospective buyers. Hence *Blue Heaven* features Ken Barnes and Roy Clarke from the 1950s through to Ian Brightwell and Niall Quinn from the present team.

I have to say that I have suffered many taunts and jibes along the way from several red scallywags that I have the misfortune to know. Comments such as 'Memorable games – must be a slim book that,' and 'You haven't had a memorable game for years,' have not deterred me from the task in hand.

This book is a collection of, I believe, interesting stories, told by the players themselves, with insights and anecdotes to which the fans are not normally privy. Take for instance a drunken Tommy Booth falling out of a taxi and Roy Clarke's potentially violent mother. Stories like these were exactly the kind of thing I was looking for – and I was delighted when I received them from every single player concerned.

With the exception of Mike Summerbee, apart from the occasional autograph I had not met any of the players prior to the commencement of this project. To a man, every one of them gave me 100 per cent support as well as their valuable time. As a fan I feel privileged to have been granted these interviews (and to have held the medals and shirts of yesteryear), and hopefully the book gives a true picture of the players' memories. There were some comments I was asked specifically not to put in the book and hopefully all of these have been omitted. These comments will form the basis of my next book – lawyers permitting. (No, no, only joking, lads!)

Prior to speaking to the players, I had in my mind the game I thought they would choose. I was wrong on seven of the 12 occasions. Before reading the book fully (hopefully that was your intention, and you're not just lurking in a bookshop waiting for the rain to stop), I would like to ask you to try the same exercise. Mind you, when you think of all the many thousands of games these players have taken part in, I don't think five correct answers is a bad score!

What this book isn't is a Manchester City 'dream team'. To pick such a team is, in my opinion, an impossible task. Perhaps the only position that every City fan would agree on would be that of manager. Without a shadow of a doubt, the late, great Joe Mercer would run the side. All the other places would surely be up for grabs. Just look at some of the great City players not included in the pages of this book: Bert Trautmann, Rodney Marsh, Dennis Tueart, Georgiou Kinkladze, Chairman Francis Lee . . . should they be in? If so, who shouldn't? I honestly don't know. If *Blue Heaven* proves as popular as *The Maine Road Encyclopedia* then these players might be in another book in the future.

What do you think, Bill?

1

JOE CORRIGAN

City v. Tottenham Hotspur
Centenary FA Cup final at Wembley Stadium, 9 May 1981

In more than 100 years of football, only one man has played more games for Manchester City than goalkeeper Joe Corrigan. Alan Oakes is the man keeping Joe off the top spot, having taken part in 665 (+4) games to Joe's 592. Looking at the appearances table I think it is reasonably safe to say that Corrigan will never be displaced from that number two position.

Of all those games played, one in particular stands out in Big Joe's mind: 'The Centenary FA Cup final of 1981. I won *The Sun*'s Man of the Match award for Saturday's game, and then in the replay on Thursday I won the BBC's Man of the Final trophy.'

That 1980–81 season had certainly been an eventful one: 'There'd been a lot of changes that year,' Joe remembers. 'We hadn't started off well with Malcolm and then John Bond came in. From then on I think we had the best record in the league – we went about 17 or 18 games without being beaten. We also got to the semi-final of the League Cup where we were beaten by Liverpool. We lost 1–0 at Maine Road and then drew 1–1 at Anfield but gave a good account of ourselves in both legs. Then of course there was the good cup run.

'Looking back, Malcolm wanted to do his own things when he returned. He put a lot of youngsters into the side all at once. The team struggled for two seasons under Malcolm and of course he still had this thing about Steve Daley. I wasn't around when the deal was completed so I don't know who had the final say-so but there were lots of rumours flying around at the time.

'Malcolm got rid of players like Asa Hartford, Gary Owen and Dave Watson – all great players. I don't want to get into a slanging match with Malcolm – after all he was the manager and that was what he wanted to do – but with me being club captain I felt I had to say certain things to him about his decisions. People told me what they wanted to happen but when I went in to see the manager these people turned around and denied saying anything. It ended up that it was always a confrontation between me and Malcolm.

'To this day I always say Malcolm was a great coach and I will never say otherwise. As a manager, though, you do have to wonder. I think the ideal job for Malcolm was running the School of Excellence at Lilleshall. If he could have been in charge there – worked with the kids, used his coaching skills – I think he would have been a great success.'

Bond's arrival and the signings of Gerry Gow, Tommy Hutchison and Bobby McDonald sparked a Maine Road revival. 'Apart from these three signings the rest of the side had been Malcolm's,' recalls Corrigan. 'John Bond was a really good man motivator, and a good coach. From day one he told us what he wanted and set about it his way – and every single day of the week we worked and worked and worked on what he wanted us to do. The dividends paid off, culminating in the League Cup semi-final and the FA Cup final.'

In typical quirky footballing fashion, City's first opponents in the FA Cup that season were Crystal Palace, managed by the recently deposed Maine Road boss Malcolm Allison. City won 4–0, and won even more comfortably in the next round when Norwich City were crushed 6–0.

'We then beat Peterborough 1–0 away,' remembers Corrigan. 'After that we beat Everton 3–1 after drawing 2–2 there and then Ipswich in the semi-final. There were some good games that season – I particularly remember the 3–1 against Everton as a cracker. We scored a lot of goals in the first two games and then I think we showed our mettle against Peterborough. It was a difficult ground to go to but Tommy Booth got the winner for us.'

That game at Peterborough brought back memories of an ill-fated

FA Cup tie the previous year: 'Oh yes, the days of Halifax! Stories going around then said "The Americans have spent ten million pounds and gone to the moon. Malcolm spent seven million and couldn't get past Halifax!"

'Games like those are always difficult. The big clubs are on a hiding to nothing – they're always expected to win. The lower division clubs throw caution to the wind. It's like their cup final and they're the only side who'll ever get anything out of it. If they win they're giantkillers – if they get beat so what, it was expected. But that's the aura of the FA Cup. That's what makes it such a special tournament.'

For the final John Bond kept faith with the side that had triumphed over Ipswich Town in the semi-final. This meant that David Bennett kept his place at number seven instead of the more experienced (and previous Wembley winner) Dennis Tueart. Ray Ranson played with stitches in a mouth wound and the pairing of Nicky Reid and Tommy Caton in the centre of defence was believed to be the youngest ever in that position for a Wembley final. City also had the oldest player on the pitch in Tommy Hutchison. What a bearing he was to have on the outcome of the 1981 FA Cup final.

Spurs were delighted to have one of their Argentinian World Cup stars, Ricardo Villa, back in their starting line-up. He had been out of the side for two months due to injury and only returned to the first team for their semi-final with Wolves. What a bearing he too would have on the game.

Sheffield referee Keith Hackett started proceedings with a blow of his Italian police whistle and Spurs began the game the faster of the two sides. Future England coach Glenn Hoddle produced the first incident when his shot from outside the box was well saved by Corrigan. Two sliding tackles by Nicky Reid broke up the next Spurs attack before Ranson was penalised for a foul on Crooks. From Perryman's free-kick Roberts forced Corrigan to make another save as Crooks followed the ball in. City's opening attack followed good work by Paul Power on the left wing. His low cross found its way to Bennett whose shot hit Roberts and went behind for a corner. From the ensuing corner Power's back-header was almost converted by full-back Bobby McDonald, always a danger at set pieces.

A good direct run by Galvin saw him unleash a low, left-foot shot which looked as though it was destined to give Spurs the lead. Joe

Corrigan had other ideas. The tallest player ever to play for the Blues hurled his 6ft 4½ins frame to his left and tipped the ball around the post.

The cup final was already living up to pre-match expectations – all that was needed now was that all-important first goal. On the half hour it was City who got it – albeit from a fairly unusual source. David Bennett battled for possession inside the Spurs half and the ball was played wide to the right and Kevin Reeves. He laid it back to Ranson who – under the manager's instructions to 'get the ball in their box quickly' – crossed it first time. Tommy Hutchison met the cross with a spectacular diving header and the ball flew past the diving Aleksic. The City fans directly behind the goal erupted.

In the previous year's FA Cup final West Ham United's number ten Trevor Brooking had scored a goal with his head. With all due respect to both players, neither Brooking nor Hutchison could be classed in the same category of headers of the ball as, say, Wyn Davies or Niall Quinn. The odds against that happening must have been several thousand to one and provides just another example of a remarkable footballing coincidence.

The Blues nearly extended their lead moments later when a shot from Reeves hit the side netting. The Tottenham defence spent the next few seconds in heated discussion about who should be marking whom. Hutchison's goal had certainly unsettled them.

A poor back-pass by Nicky Reid almost provided Crooks with the equaliser but once again Corrigan came to the rescue with a brave diving save on the edge of the area. 'I remember that collision,' says Corrigan today. 'I thought at first I'd broken a finger but fortunately I'd just started wearing gloves and I got away with it.' The Blues' faithful greeted this save with a rousing chorus of 'England's Number One.'

More incidents were to follow in the last minute of the half. Appeals for a Spurs penalty were turned down when Galvin ran into Ranson, Reeves collided with goalkeeper Aleksic and Roberts was kicked in the face by fellow defender Hughton. (Aleksic and Roberts had both been to Wembley before, Aleksic in 1972 when he helped Stafford Rangers to victory in the FA Trophy and Roberts 12 months later – as a ballboy during Sunderland's famous defeat of the all-powerful Leeds United.)

Spurs began the second half in the same positive way as they'd started the first. Crooks was flattened by Caton near the corner flag just moments before the same player almost scored his 22nd goal of the season. Fortunately for City his cross-shot went wide of the target.

Ardiles produced his first piece of skill of the afternoon as Tottenham continued the pressure. He played a one-two with Crooks but was blocked by McDonald at the expense of a corner. Corrigan held the corner safely and was trodden on by Miller for his trouble. Fine build-up play at the other end put MacKenzie through on goal with only the keeper to beat but the City player was unable to control the ball properly and his left-foot shot hit the outside of the post.

Having found it difficult to make any impression on the game, Ricardo Villa now found himself replaced by substitute Gary Brooke. It was a disgruntled figure that left the play, probably thinking about his family back home who were watching the game live on television. What a difference five days would make!

Brooke was immediately in the thick of the action, forcing Corrigan to block a shot. Such was the side's commitment, the City goalkeeper was just one of six defenders inside the six-yard area at the time of Brooke's effort.

With just ten minutes left Gow lost the ball to Ardiles and in his haste to regain possession, fouled the Argentinian just outside City's penalty area. Hoddle's free-kick hit Tommy Hutchison and the ball was deflected past the helpless Corrigan. It was perhaps the only way the ball could have got past him all afternoon.

City's number one recalls the incident: 'The way that goal came about actually reared its head on the Thursday before the game. We were having a training session near the hotel in Selsdon Park. John Bond was talking us through defensive tactics for free-kicks and corners – it was something we always did.

'Because of the ability of Glenn Hoddle to bend the ball, John Bond came up with the idea of dropping Tommy Hutchison back onto the goal-line. Nowadays this is fairly common – it's a way, if you like, of trying to force the kicker to play to one side of the goal or the other. Anyway we discussed it at length and I said I didn't want that to happen.

'No disrespect to Tommy, but he's a forward not a defender. Let defenders defend and let the forwards be part of the wall. If people start walking backwards and forwards, not only could it distract me from my job, it could also distract him from his. Tommy Booth and Tommy Caton both agreed with me and in the end we decided against it. We'd not played this way in previous games and Hutch himself wasn't keen either.

'On the day of the game – I think there was only about ten minutes to go – they got a free-kick and Tommy overheard them talking about what they were going to do. As he was walking back to join the wall and Hoddle, Perryman and Ardiles were lining up the kick, Tommy heard Hoddle say he was going to bend it round to my left. Because of this, just before the kick Tommy decides he'll drop off the wall. The unfortunate thing about the goal was that if he'd stood up straight, and not tried to get out of the way, the ball would have hit him square and bounced away. But because he tried to get out of the way, the ball struck him somewhere up near his shoulder and deflected into the corner. I had no chance – I was flying through the air with the greatest of ease towards the other corner!

'At the time people thought we were just happy to sit on our one goal lead and wait for the final whistle. But we weren't that kind of team and John Bond wasn't that kind of manager. Just before their goal Steve MacKenzie broke through; the ball bobbled, hit him on the shin and then hit the post. If that had gone in we'd have won the Cup. It didn't go in, and who knows, it might have just geed the Spurs players up a little. They may have thought: "This isn't over yet – we've still got a chance."

'The day we were going to win it was the Saturday. We were never going to win it on the Thursday. It wasn't meant to be – our name just wasn't on it.' Tottenham's was – if for no other reason than the year ended with a number one.

Hutchison's unfortunate feat would for ever keep his name in the record books. He is one of only two players ever to score for both teams in a Wembley FA Cup final. In 1946 Charlton Athletic's right-half Bert Turner scored at both ends inside a minute and would also finish the game on the losing side – Derby County winning the game 4–1 after extra-time.

The last incident of the 90 minutes of Wembley 1981 also involved Hutchison when his low cross from the right was turned into the side netting by Steve MacKenzie. The final score of 1–1 meant that a further half-hour would be played. It was the first time since Arsenal beat Liverpool back in 1971 that extra-time would be required to settle an FA Cup final.

Both City and Tottenham had played extra-time in their respective semi-finals but here at Wembley the further 30 minutes only produced cramp as opposed to the deciding goal. The nearest either side came to scoring in the first period was a 20-yard effort from Tottenham substitute Brooke which flew over the crossbar. Players on both sides were now suffering with the infamous Wembley cramp and it came as no surprise when Tony Henry's fresh legs replaced Tommy Hutchison's exhausted ones at the interval.

More of the same followed in the second period. Glenn Hoddle was down with the aforementioned cramp and was a prone spectator as Gow shot wide following a good cross from Reeves. Aleksic snatched the ball off Power's head just moments before referee Keith Hackett blew his whistle for the last time as Reeves and Miller were jockeying for possession near the corner flag.

It was only the second Wembley draw after extra-time (the first being Chelsea versus Leeds United in 1970) and it would be the first ever FA Cup final to be replayed at Wembley.

In a most peculiar situation both teams were presented to Her Majesty the Queen Mother without a cup or medal on show. Paul Power led the side on a somewhat subdued lap of honour with Corrigan consoling and managing at last to put a smile on the still-dejected face of Tommy Hutchison.

Joe Corrigan has his own opinions of drawn FA Cup finals: 'I'm a great believer in finishing the game on the Saturday. The FA Cup final is such a great event and I think it loses something when it is finished on a Thursday. Also it's not fair on the supporters. Our fans had to travel home, then travel back, and with the tickets being on sale on Monday morning, it meant there was something like 50,000 Spurs fans in the ground for the replay. The other thing as well is the cost; a lot of our fans simply couldn't afford the trip again. I always think the game should be settled on the day with play continuing until somebody scores.'

For the Tottenham players, the replay would be their ninth FA Cup game of the season. For their supporters it would be their eighth FA Cup game played in the capital. Economics were not as important to Londoners as they were to Mancunians.

The game on the Thursday produced five goals, one of which seemingly overshadows almost every other scored at the world-famous Empire Stadium. Not, however, in the eyes of Joe Corrigan: 'Everyone says the last goal – probably because it was the winner – was a great goal, but there was a catalogue of errors leading up to it. Admittedly, Villa had tremendous skill and certainly did the business, but we should never have let him get that far.

'As far as I'm concerned the goal of the game was Steve MacKenzie's. The ball was laid off by Tommy Hutchison and it was a tremendous volley from outside the box. That for me took great skill. Every time the FA Cup starts in January the television companies show that Villa goal. I'm reminded of it every year – I'm sick of it! I always thought the score was 3–2 but now I reckon it was 56–2, the number of times I've seen it.'

He continues: 'We'd gone behind after seven minutes. I blocked a shot from Archibald and Villa scored from the rebound. We then went 2–1 up through Steve MacKenzie's great strike and Kevin Reeves' penalty. I think at that moment we should have gone for it; we should have brought Dennis Tueart on. With hindsight now we sat back a little and let them come at us. We just got overrun in midfield. Dennis did come on but it was too late then, we were 3–2 down. He came on for Bobby McDonald. If he'd come on when we were leading – an extra attacker – Spurs would have had to have thought more about defending than they actually did.'

The Saturday game was the first time Corrigan had played at Wembley in an FA Cup final. He had, however, played in two League Cup finals in 1970 and 1976, missing out to Keith MacRae in the 1974 defeat by Wolves.

Is there a difference between playing in an FA Cup final and a League Cup final? According to Corrigan, 'Yes, there is. I remember the first time I'd been to Wembley, back in 1970 against West Bromwich Albion. I got off the coach and Malcolm Allison says to me: "I don't want you to go to the dressing-room just yet. I want you to go up the tunnel – on your own – and just stand in the middle of the pitch."

'At first I wondered what he was talking about but as I was just a kid of 21 I did as I was told. There is something there you have to go through – I can't really describe it. It's like a curtain I suppose – a curtain of atmosphere. It put me in good stead and I did it in 1976 when Tony Book was manager and again with John Bond. In the League Cups it's usually a League official or similar who is there on the day. But for the FA Cup it's always a member of the Royal Family. That for me makes the day a bit more special. I remember the Queen Mother was at ours in 1981 and of course we all got a chance to meet her. That was an experience for me – she's a lovely woman.

'It's little things like that that make it different for me. It's a package. The whole day goes so quickly really and you don't take everything in at the time. Thank goodness there's video nowadays. I've got tapes of the games and when I watch them I think: "How did that happen?" and "Oh yes, I remember that." It's great to be able to look back at them.'

I asked Joe if that solitary Wembley walk was a Corrigan superstition, to which he replied 'No, not really, it was just something Malcolm made me do that first time. I wouldn't have done it on my own. It was his way of telling me that some of the game's greatest players had frozen because of the intense Wembley atmosphere and had had poor games.

'Having said that though, I was a very superstitious player. When I got back in the side in 1975, "Big Helen" Turner would always give me a sprig of heather before every single game. When we won the League Cup in 1976 I wore the same clothes for every match and would always take them off in exactly the same way. It's just a routine you get into and if it seems to be working, well then you don't change it. When I was having a bad time – during the 1972–73 season for instance – if something went right for me I just tried to keep it going.'

Back to Wembley in 1981, Joe has other recollections and observations: 'I remember in the first game the lads played really well. I honestly don't think we could have played any better but we were conned out of the replay. There was so much in the press about Gerry Gow and his handling of Ardiles. Certainly he'd rattled him a couple of times but Gerry was playing his usual way – the only way he knew. The Spurs players had said things in the press and on the Thursday they were constantly going on to Keith Hackett about Gerry's tackling. He gave them a lot more in the second game than he did in the first.

'I don't think this made Gerry play badly, but it certainly put him on his guard. He was also suffering with his knees and his ankles and it was asking a lot of him to play two important, hard games in the space of a few days. It just goes back to what I said before about finishing the game on the Saturday.

'I don't agree with a penalty shoot-out, but I do like the American way of "next goal wins". Sure, some people might say the players would be dropping like flies, but that's what actually happened in extra-time on Saturday anyway. The fitter team at the end of the day would win. The fans would definitely stay on and it would make great television.' (Joe Corrigan was interviewed for this book on 29 April 1996, just days before that unfortunate 2–2 draw with Liverpool, and some three months prior to the 'next goal wins' events of Euro 96.)

At the time Joe was winning the Man of the Final trophy – but unfortunately not the FA Cup – he was living in Sale, where he was born and bred. 'My uncle Tom was the only real what you would call footballer in the family,' he recalls. 'It was actually him who pushed me down the road to play. As a 14 year-old I played open age football in the Altrincham and District Saturday League – always as a goalkeeper. Ever since I was about four or five I'd wanted to be a keeper. It was never a case of "He's too big to play out, he'll have to go in goal" – I always wanted to go in goal. Every chance I had I would be goalkeeper and would get really upset when I had to play out! During my school days at Sale Grammar we played a lot of rugby so on Saturday mornings I played rugby and then the open age football in the afternoons.

'I left school to go to AEI in Trafford Park where I joined the training school. We used to have these inter-departmental games and in this one particular game I was playing centre-half. At half-time I went in goal and later on this guy came up to me and asked me if I'd like a trial. I said "Who for?" and he said he'd write to both Manchester United and Manchester City. I said "Fair enough", and to be honest I never thought any more about it. This guy wasn't a scout and had no connections with either club, he just worked for AEI and was watching the game. I can't remember his name though!

'A couple of weeks later I left the training school and began to work in the same department as this guy. One day he gave me a letter telling me to attend a trial at Maine Road the following Thursday.

Apparently this guy had played in goal for the British Army and so he knew his stuff. Fortunately for me Harry Godwin took note and sent for me. It was at the time when Joe and Malcolm were looking out for young Manchester-based players so I went along for the trial. I passed the trial and they signed me from Sale that same evening. I often wondered why they signed me so quickly. Harry Godwin never told me and then one day it clicked: they found out I was having a trial with United the following week. Maybe that's what swung it for me. I was very lucky really, because there's no way a situation like that would happen today. I have to admit I was a Red in those days but I soon changed my mind!'

Just over a year later Joe Corrigan was in goal for the first time in Manchester City's senior side. It was a game played at Maine Road on 11 October 1967: 'Against Blackpool in the League Cup. We drew 1–1. They had quite a good side out – Jimmy Armfield, Gordon Milne and Ray Charnley played – and the first time I went near the ball it went through my legs and John Craven scored. Fortunately for us Mike Summerbee equalised a couple of minutes later and we went on to win the replay 2–0.'

Was it the worst moment of Joe's long and distinguished career? 'No, and it wasn't even the goal scored by Ronnie Boyce either. If you look at that I think it was one hell of a shot by him rather than a ridiculous mistake by me.

'Apart from when City bought Keith MacRae and I thought my days were numbered, the worst moments during the 17 years I spent at Maine Road were when my parents got abuse for the mistakes I made. Players today are under even more pressure than during my time but the irony of the situation is that nobody ever says anything to the players directly. More often than not, though, I would find out and it hurt.

'If anything it perhaps made me more determined to succeed and so prove them wrong. My parents were both ordinary, working Manchester people and fortunately they were big enough to take it. They were certainly bigger and better people than those dishing it out. In the end I played First Division football and nine times for England. I achieved all that with an awful lot of determination.'

He also remembers another unpleasant occasion after he'd left Maine Road: 'The other sad thing was when I was playing for

Brighton. We were playing City in a Second Division game at Maine Road and after the game this guy comes up to me and calls me a traitor. I took no notice and just walked straight past him but people don't know what happened when I left Manchester City.

'I went to Seattle Sounders of the NASL in March 1983 and people thought I was just going for the money. But I knew after we'd lost 4–0 in the FA Cup at Brighton in the January that I was on my way. After the game I said to Alex Williams, "You'll be in soon." I knew that, because of the wages I was on as one of the senior players, I wouldn't be there much longer.

'It then came out in the press that Seattle were interested in me. Mr Swales called a meeting and asked me what was going on. I said, "What do you mean, what's going on, it's been in the papers for the last month." He denied all knowledge, saying he knew nothing at all. In the end I asked him if he wanted me to go or stay. He replied, "I'll leave that up to you." I said, "Mr Chairman, that's the first time you've ever said that to me. Every other time there's been a team in for me you've told me I'm not going. You want me to go." He said: "No, no – it's not like that." When I left, I think City were either 15th or 16th and about 11 points clear of the relegation zone. But after 17 years' service – not all of them good because I did take an awful lot of flak – for someone to turn round and call me a traitor, that really did hurt a lot.'

Corrigan played for six months in the United States – just the one season – before moving back to England with Brighton in September. 'The manager of Seattle Sounders was a guy called Laurie Calloway and he was very friendly with Jimmy Melia, manager of Brighton at the time.

'Seattle were folding but trying to get an indoor side together and they needed to bring some money into the club. I suppose I was the only asset they had and so they sold me. I played for Brighton for two years and had a couple of loan spells at Stoke and Norwich. I retired in 1986 – had to really. I got injured playing for Brighton against Queen's Park Rangers on the astroturf at Loftus Road. I went out to scoop the ball up – you couldn't slide out because of the risk of burns – and was up-ended by their forward. I landed heavily and a disc squeezed out and paralysed my left side. I needed an operation to have a bone put in my neck.

'I suppose in a way I was lucky. I was 30 when it happened yet it could so easily have happened when I was 20. The specialist told me there was a danger if I got another knock on it the bone could flake away and move backwards. That would completely ruin my spinal column, but – touch wood – I've had no trouble with it since. I still dive about like an idiot!'

After his injury, Joe moved back up north to Macclesfield to set up a haulage business with a friend. Unfortunately this didn't work out as planned but fate was just around the corner, as Joe explains: 'I was working for a subsidiary company of TNT Parcels in their import/export department. One day after work I stopped off at the local golf club for a drink on the way home.

'There'd been a *Manchester Evening News* Pro/Am tournament on and Howard Kendall was there. He asked me what I was doing and would I like to come back to Maine Road to start goalkeeping coaching. He thought it would be good for the club. Just minutes later Mel Machin walked in. He was in charge at Barnsley but was still living nearby. We had the same conversation and he offered me a job. A few days after these two job offers I got a third when Colin Todd rang me from Middlesbrough. It was amazing how quickly the word had got around!

'But for that chance conversation with Howard Kendall I don't think I would ever have got into coaching. Funnily enough though it was probably something I'd always wanted to do. I worked so hard at my game with Roy Bailey, Tony Book, Glyn Pardoe and Malcolm Allison but I always thought it would have been great to have someone like Bert Trautmann, even just to talk to.

'Bert was at that West Ham game when Ronnie Boyce scored and he said to me, "Don't worry about it – I've let in far worse goals than that. People will forget. Just put it behind you." If I'd had Bert there all the time to talk to when I needed to, I'm sure it would have helped. That's part of the goalkeeping coach's brief. Goalkeeping is such a specialist job, and confidence and motivation play big parts.'

In May 1992 Joe Corrigan was one of many people who left Maine Road as the victims of Peter Reid's organisational changes. 'Peter and Sam Ellis decided they didn't need a goalkeeping coach. They were the managers and they made the decisions but I have to say I was upset and disappointed. After Maine Road I did part-time work at Leeds,

Barnsley, Bradford and Celtic. I got all those jobs by word-of-mouth and eventually I was offered a full-time position at Anfield about two years ago. I love it there and it's a great club to work for.'

Although nowadays his priorities quite rightly lie with Liverpool, he still has a soft spot for City, saying: 'I spent 17 years of my life there so it's not something I'm going to forget easily. It's been 20 years now since City won anything and I think that's tragic. For my money things began to go wrong at Maine Road when Tony Book was sacked as manager. He'd been there a long time and knew everything and everybody. Continuity is a great thing in football – just look at Liverpool.

'I just hope it's not another 20 years before City win a trophy.'

Saturday, 9 May 1981

Centenary FA Cup final at Wembley Stadium

Manchester City	1	(Hutchison)
Tottenham Hotspur	1	(Hutchison o.g.)

MANCHESTER CITY	v.	TOTTENHAM HOTSPUR
Joe Corrigan	1	Milija Aleksic
Ray Ranson	2	Chris Hughton
Bobby McDonald	3	Paul Miller
Nicky Reid	4	Graham Roberts
Paul Power	5	Steve Perryman
Tommy Caton	6	Ricardo Villa*
David Bennett	7	Osvaldo Ardiles
Gerry Gow	8	Steve Archibald
Steve MacKenzie	9	Tony Galvin
*Tommy Hutchison	10	Glenn Hoddle
Kevin Reeves	11	Garth Crooks
*Tony Henry	SUB	Garry Brooke*

Attendance: 99,500

2

IAN BRIGHTWELL

City v. Manchester United
Football League Division One at Maine Road, 23 September 1989

During the 1970s, Lancashire County Cricket Club had a solid middle-order batsman by the name of Frank Hayes. Having made his debut in 1970 as a 23 year-old, Hayes was affectionately known as 'Young Frank'. He would carry this tag with him for 14 years until his enforced retirement, due to a brittle-bone condition, in 1984.

A similar thing could be said about Ian Brightwell.

Brightwell signed associate schoolboy forms for City in September 1982, turning professional on 3 May 1986. It is perhaps hard to believe that 'Young Ian' or 'Bob' is now in his 11th year as a professional footballer. During that time he has seen relegation, promotion, FA Youth Cup success and (including one caretaker) eight managers.

Born in the Leicestershire town of Lutterworth on 9 April 1968, Ian is the son of former British athletes Robbie Brightwell and Anne Packer. I asked him how he came to move up to Manchester. 'My dad was a lecturer at Loughborough College, and then got a job with Adidas,' he told me. 'He was asked to set up Adidas UK – it was already well known in Germany – and so we moved up to Poynton to establish the UK headquarters. Although Adidas was based in Poynton, we actually lived in Congleton. I'd have been two and a half

35

or three at the time.' (Even today the Brightwells live in Congleton, although Ian now has his own place – just around the corner from his parents.)

A fine middle-distance runner at school, Brightwell was discovered by City at a soccer coaching school in Macclesfield. 'It was a bit like the Bobby Charlton ones nowadays – a privately run one. A guy called Barry Bennell spotted me and asked me to come down to City for trials.' (Bennell was indirectly employed by City and ran the nursery sides for the club.)

Brightwell continued, 'It just went from there really. At the time there was myself, Andy Hinchcliffe, Steve Redmond, David White and Paul Lake all in the same team. This was the nucleus of the side that won the FA Youth Cup in 1986, and we'd all played together since we were about 12. Everyone knew everyone else's strengths and weaknesses.'

Positions were slightly different then though: 'Steve Redmond was centre-forward – a good one as well – and Andy Hinchcliffe was left-wing.' Little did they know that these five talented schoolboys would all play key roles in Ian Brightwell's most memorable game some nine years later.

It was during these schoolboy days that Brightwell was christened with the nickname 'Bob', a nickname he still has at the club today. 'Steve Redmond started that off. It's from my dad really, and it's also my middle name. We were just messing around one day – I was calling him Tony because his dad is called Tony. He came back with Bob because of my dad and it just stuck. I quite like it actually.'

Following his debut against Wimbledon at Maine Road on 23 August 1986, Brightwell became City's 'Mr Versatility'. That season he wore various numbered shirts, all associated with attacking positions. The following season, 1987–88, saw him wearing mainly defensive numbers, with five being the most-used. Today Brightwell confesses to preferring either five or two, but has actually played in every position except goalkeeper for the Blues' first team. When Trevor Morley's goal at Bradford City on 13 May 1989 ensured First Division football would return to Maine Road the following season, Brightwell was wearing his favourite number five shirt.

With First Division football come two vitally important dates; the home and away fixtures of the Manchester derby. Ian Brightwell remembers the Maine Road clash on 23 September 1989: 'It was hot, very hot, the middle of September – and everybody I knew was after tickets. There was a big crowd and it was the first derby since our 2–0 defeat at Old Trafford back in March 1987.' This would be the third time 'Bob' had played against United and he had yet to be on the winning side. His first appearance came as a substitute replacement for Tony Grealish in a 1–1 draw at Maine Road in October 1986 (Ireland manager Mick McCarthy scored City's equaliser that day), and his second in that March 1987 clash.

The Blues' return to the First Division had also produced their worst start to a season for nine years. They went into the game propping up the division along with Sheffield Wednesday and Tottenham, their four points from six games made up of a draw with Tottenham and a win against Queen's Park Rangers.

United, on the other hand were still celebrating a Mark Hughes hat-trick in the 5–1 defeat of league leaders Millwall the previous weekend, and had a host of big-name and big-money players in the side. Gary Pallister (£2.3 million), Paul Ince (£1.7 million), Danny Wallace (£1.2 million) and Mike Phelan (£750,000) were up against what was largely City's Second Division side, which in turn was the successful youth side of three years earlier. United's captain Bryan Robson, always a key figure and big influence, missed the game with a shin injury. Mike Phelan took his place as captain, whilst the honour of leading out the Blues fell to the former Wimbledon player Brian Gayle.

City had not beaten United since 1981, and were trailing 33 matches to 39 in the 110 league derbies played. On a positive note for the Blues, United had conceded ten goals in their opening six matches and had yet to keep a clean sheet.

For United only Mark Hughes and Mike Duxbury had experienced Manchester derbies before, and Brian McClair played in a headband with seven stitches in a wound on his forehead. On the City side, David White, Steve Redmond and Ian Brightwell had played in previous derbies, although Brightwell probably wouldn't have played in this one except for the illness which kept Neil McNab on the sidelines. In goal for the Blues was the 35-year-old Paul Cooper, the oldest player on the pitch, now in his 18th season in professional football. Cooper had signed from Leicester City six months previously and replaced the injured Andy Dibble.

The odds were stacked heavily in United's favour, but by 5 p.m. on the eighth anniversary of Bill Shankly's death, the football world would know differently. Ian Brightwell recalls: 'Never in my wildest dreams could I have imagined what happened. Everyone thought we had a chance, and none of us had ever seen so many people in Maine Road before. The whole afternoon was amazing.'

For City this was to be manager Mel Machin's one and only Manchester derby. For United it was Alex Ferguson's second, it could so easily have been his last.It was a hot day, and the crowd – many dressed in the sunglasses, hats and short-sleeves normally associated with cricket – settled down to watch United begin the game brightly.

Minutes into the game crowd trouble forced fans onto the pitch, prompting referee Neil Midgley – in his first Manchester derby – to take the teams off the pitch for a period of eight minutes.

'Perhaps this disturbance upset United's concentration,' remembers Brightwell today. It certainly didn't upset City's.Within minutes of the restart Morley was fouled by Beardsmore just inside United's half. Andy Hinchcliffe fired the free-kick across the field to the right-wing and David White. He in turn ran at the United full-back Duxbury (wearing number four), before pulling back a low cross into the penalty area. The £2.3 million Gary Pallister was unable to reach it and the ball rolled to City's Australian-born David Oldfield who hooked it high into the net past the diving Jim Leighton.

Before the celebrations had died down, City were two goals up. Another cross by White – this time aimed towards the charging Brightwell – was intercepted by Ince. Donaghy's attempted clearance was charged down by Trevor Morley whose shot was parried across goal by Leighton. The ball ran across Brightwell to the left-hand side of the area to Lake who shot again. (At this point Brightwell was standing, in space, arms outstretched, waiting for a simple pass back into the centre.)

Once again Leighton parried, only this time Trevor Morley – despite the presence of several red shirts – reacted quickest and managed to poke the ball home. The photographs taken of this goal show Morley in a position not dissimilar to the one he was in when he scored that vital goal at Bradford.

Understandably, at this point City paused for breath, took their collective foot off the gas and sat back a little. United began to get back into the match and played some good, if not too penetrating, football.

David White was having a fine game for City, his storming runs and crosses causing countless difficulties in the United defence. Brightwell himself almost increased City's lead further when he just failed to connect with one of these crosses as he slid into the six-yard box. Moments later, with the first of many choruses of 'What a waste of money' echoing round the ground, another White cross went skidding across the gaping United goal.

At the other end Hinchcliffe cleared two corners off the line. For a neutral spectator (if there is such a thing in the ground on derby day), it was a fantastic match, played at a pace which it was surely not possible to maintain for the whole 90 minutes.

In the 35th minute the game was all but over. Wallace's pass was cut out by Steve Redmond who played a short one-two with Paul Lake. Redmond then sent David Oldfield – not White this time – away down the right. Oldfield beat the sliding tackle of Pallister and played a low cross into the penalty area where the ball was met by Ian Bishop's spectacular diving header and City led 3–0. David White and 'Bob' Brightwell were first on the scene to congratulate the scorer.

Not one person in the crowd of 43,246 could believe it. All the blue throats in the stadium were by now red and and voices were hoarse, whilst the United fans began cries of 'Ferguson out'. What would have happened at Old Trafford if Chairman Martin Edwards – himself under threat from businessman Michael Knighton at the time – had heeded that advice? Television commentator Clive Tyldesley remarked on Brightwell 'having a terrific match' in his attacking midfield role, although the player himself modestly says otherwise. 'Everyone played well and everything we did came off,' he claims.

The half-time break came and went seemingly in a matter of seconds. Within five minutes of the second half starting, a flying volley from Mark Hughes pulled a goal back for United. This goal began a good spell for United, during which time Paul Cooper made a fine diving save from Wallace.

Had the tide turned?

Could the unthinkable happen?

No, it couldn't – could it?

Even Brightwell was having similar thoughts at the time: 'My mind went back to the previous season when we played Bournemouth at Maine Road. We were 3–0 up at half-time and finished up drawing 3–3. I thought to myself "Here we go again".'

Fortunately the Bournemouth game wasn't about to repeat itself. In the 61st minute a tackle by Ian Bishop rebounded and struck Paul Lake. Amidst appeals for handball, Lake ran on; his shot struck the legs of Leighton and ran loose. The City player stayed on his feet and knocked the ball across an empty net for David Oldfield to easily tap in his second goal of the game. It was the first time City had scored four times against United since 12 December 1970, when a Francis Lee hat-trick and a goal by Mike Doyle won the Old Trafford fixture 4–1.

After a spell of regularly being caught offside, City scored their fifth of the afternoon: a goal clinical in both approach work and finishing. Ian Bishop played a one-two with Paul Lake in the centre circle and then sent a long, curling pass into the path of David White on the right-wing. White crossed first time on the run and the ball was headed past the hapless Leighton by Andy Hinchcliffe from about ten yards out. Hinchcliffe then proceeded to remind the United followers in the Platt Lane Stand of the score by offering them an outstretched palm, fingers pointing upwards, in North American Indian 'How' fashion. All they could manage in reply was to sing once again about the club and manager parting company.

City had never scored five times before in a Maine Road derby and Hinchcliffe's goal meant the Blues moved above United in the league, albeit on goal difference. Thirty-four years earlier, back in February 1955, City had beaten United 5–0 at Old Trafford in a game where the Reds were confused into oblivion by 'The Revie Plan'.

Today Brightwell has difficulties remembering particular incidents from the game in 1989, although he will admit to remembering the goals, having seen them many times on video. 'It was over so quickly,' he recalls, 'Everyone in the side was so pumped up, full of energy. It was almost like fantasy football years before fantasy football existed.'

The *Manchester Evening News* produced a two-page full-colour special edition on the Monday following the game. In it, manager Mel Machin voiced his feelings to City reporter Peter Gardner. The article, headed by 'Oh, what a lovely feeling', read as follows:

Pride and passion won the derby for Manchester City. 'If we can play like that once, we can play like that again,' claimed Mel Machin, following City's most convincing home victory in history against their millionaire neighbours from Old Trafford.

Said Machin, 'We have set ourselves a standard and it is one we must try to maintain. I accept it would be asking too much of the team to play like that in every game, but there is no reason why they should not approach it in achieving a high standard of consistency.

'I was proud of my players. Proud of the way they approached the game and proud at the way they conducted themselves in achieving this splendid result.

'I thought we reached a standard of near perfection in the 10–1 demolition of Huddersfield Town a couple of years back. But this performance surpassed even that and it left me with a lovely feeling.

'My players didn't really need motivating for this one. We wanted to win more than they did . . . that is the simple reason for our success. We never gave United an inch of room to work in, and when we had the ball we were quick to attack them. In fact, watching a video of the game, I found it hard to believe the team was going as strong at the end as they were at the beginning.'

Machin maintained it was essentially a team performance, although he still had a particular word of praise for two-goal marksman David Oldfield. Said the City boss, 'He not only scored twice but made another goal. Oldfield and Morley, as a pair of strikers working in harmony, were first-class. But then, so were our central defenders.

'I have given the players a bit of stick recently. In previous games, we had been creating plenty of chances but not taking them. However, I always knew that one day we would catch someone. It was nice when it happened to the people across the road.'

Indeed it was. It was a richly-deserved reward for the Blues, and will give them the confidence to carry out their boss's orders as they seek to establish themselves in Division One.

The same newspaper also carried an article by United reporter David Meek. As a United follower of many years, Meek was obviously devastated by the events of the Saturday but, in his column headed 'United, this was simply a disgrace!', he gives a very honest opinion of the game:

> The best that can be said of Manchester United is that they shared in a six-goal thriller . . . but they cannot be allowed to slip off the hook that easily!
>
> The unhappy truth is that the Reds were a derby disgrace. Nothing must be taken away from Manchester City, because they were absolutely super. They played out of their skins and deserved every aspect of their thumping 5–1 victory.
>
> But from United's point of view, they offered token, puny resistance. It seemed to me they had paid too much attention to City's struggle to establish themselves in the First Division. They had noted their lean scoring spell and they believed the bookmakers' odds and form book.
>
> In other words they thought it was going to be a doddle. In fairness, I hadn't spoken to a City fan all week who seriously thought his team would win. The result was that United's high-priced superstars, most of them new to the Manchester scene, learned their first derby lesson – that the team which most wants to win generally does so.
>
> Hopefully, they will now realise that a team playing with the passion of City at Maine Road on Saturday will always come out on top against a side which cannot match such fire, regardless of their pedigree. City were quicker to the ball, and better on it when they got there. They made United's team look overpriced, overpaid and overrun. The late withdrawal of Bryan Robson didn't help. The man who really knows the Manchester derby scene and is capable of doing something about it had to pull out when it was discovered his bruised shin was, in fact, a hairline fracture.
>
> United kept it a secret until after the match, but they would have done better working out an effective plan to cover their captain's absence. Switching Mike Phelan back into midfield and playing Mal Donaghy at centre-back, with Mike Duxbury at left-back, was a disaster.

The defence had a nightmare, including the costly Gary Pallister, who thought he had come to Old Trafford to boost his international chances rather than see them destroyed.

United's manager – the shell-shocked Alex Ferguson – said 'It was the worst defensive performance in my time at United. We lost terrible goals. It was like trying to climb a glass mountain. The finishing of City was the deciding factor. Our goal should have been the signal for us to do something, but we just fell apart. I don't think Jim Leighton has ever had five goals scored against him in his life. It was just one of those days at the back.'

It wasn't much better in other places either! Every single City player earned a maximum ten in the newspaper form guides. United's average was five. Even referee Neil Midgley got a ten. Pity he's now retired – we could have him for every game! Peter Gardner continues the story of that marvellous September day:

> It was sheer Blue murder as Manchester City eclipsed their expensive neighbours in a no-contest derby. And they did so simply because they possessed a greater urgency and a burning desire for success.
>
> The Blues, once lavish spenders themselves, demonstrated effectively that money does not necessarily buy success. Manchester United were made to look sad and sorry millionaire misfits by comparison with a refreshing City side that included five players who cost the club nothing.
>
> The rest had been assembled at a modest £2m – less than the price it took the Reds to recruit Gary Pallister, whose personal nightmare paved the way for City's most crushing home derby success in history and their first for almost nine years.
>
> It was a scintillating victory, the foundations of which were built on the willingness of 11 players to contribute 100 per cent effort in a bid to recover from an unconvincing start to their First Division return.
>
> United simply could not live with a team who outran, outfought and outsmarted them in every facet of the game. Underdogs City may have been before the match, but there was no denying their superiority at the end of what was a superb,

crushing victory over a club whose image was tarnished on and off the field.

Off the field were those disgraceful scenes at the outset when referee Neil Midgley, who handled the match magnificently, took the players to the dressing-rooms for an eight-minute hold-up. The Reds supporters, who had infiltrated the North Stand City end, were marshalled to a no man's land in the Platt Lane sector reserved for the Old Trafford contingent.

On the field the Reds were run ragged, with City striking two hammer blows within 60 sensational seconds to take a grip they never relaxed.

In fact, City were maintaining the same demanding pace at the end as they had set from the start of an amazing confrontation. This was essentially a brilliant team exhibition, but there were men who deserved extra credit. And none more so than David Oldfield, who looked a £1m-plus marksman as he scored twice and figured in another goal. Not to be forgotten, either, is his willing partner Trevor Morley, whose late goal at Bradford last spring enabled City to clinch automatic promotion.

Morley and Oldfield combined to form almost the perfect partnership as they gave the hapless Pallister and company a chasing they will not easily forget.

Another pairing, too, contributed magnificently to a victory that can do much for City's morale in the demanding months ahead. Brian Gayle and Steve Redmond played the United front-runners commendably, and it took a strike of world-class proportions from Mark Hughes to score the Reds' lone goal, for which the otherwise unemployed Paul Cooper could hardly be faulted.

Ian Bishop and Ian Brightwell bossed the midfield to perfection. David White's devastating pace was never matched. Paul Lake toiled tirelessly before injury forced his departure, and Andy Hinchcliffe and Gary Fleming made telling goal-line clearances on the few occasions United did threaten. Hinchcliffe, too, crowned his effort with a fifth goal as he came from nowhere to head in a rocket-like effort from one of many quality White crosses.

This, then, is City at their brilliant best. The hope now is that they can continue to play in the same positive manner to achieve respectability beyond that gained here.

Beautiful memories. I'm not certain which I've seen more – 'City 5 United 1' or *The Great Escape.*

Perhaps the only black spot on that day was when Paul Lake left the pitch with an injured knee, his place being taken by Jason Beckford. Now, seven years later, following the tragic injury-forced retirement of Lake, Ian Brightwell is the sole member of that side still at Maine Road.

Casting his eye over photographs of the goals, 'Bob's' comments are: 'The first one, Gary Pallister slipped over trying to cut the ball out; the second one Trevor Morley poked it in; the third, Stevie Redmond played it wide to David Oldfield and a great header from Ian Bishop. Lakey cut that one back for four-one – and that was a great ball in from David White.' The greatest derby day in living memory summed up in just those few short words!

'It was a great day,' he continues, 'not just for me but for the fans as well, for everyone. It was a great team performance. Right from the back with Paul Cooper. Although he didn't have much to do in the game, he just kept us going, shouting encouragement all the time. He was a great talker.'

Praise also for full-back Gary Fleming: 'Another fine performance, up against the skills of Danny Wallace. Very solid, made some great tackles. Everyone played out of their skins.'

Of all the goals, Brightwell particularly remembers the fourth: 'This one sticks in my mind more than the others. When Lakey got the ball he set himself for a shot, and then just cut it back from the by-line for David Oldfield. I forget who the defender was [It was Mike Duxbury], but he went sliding in, missed it, and Oldfield just tapped it in. I always remember Clive Tyldesley saying on TV "and I could have scored that". Full marks for Lakey – he really made that goal.'

After the game a club owner friend of 'Bob's' presented him with a magnum of champagne with which to celebrate. 'We soon finished that off,' he told me, 'and we had one or two shandies as well'. Headlines such as 'Maine Road Massacre' and 'Blue Murder' filled the newspapers in the days that followed. By 'eck, it was even more great than normal to be a Blue that particular weekend!

If City have just one survivor from that game, then United have three: Gary Pallister, Brian McClair and substitute Lee Sharpe. The only other constant is United manager Alex Ferguson.

Brightwell gives his honest opinions on that score: 'During the game United's fans were shouting for Ferguson's head and yet look what's happened since. I think you have to give managers a chance, you can't go sacking them here, there and everywhere. You have to give all managers a fair run. Everyone will have bad times, but you have to stick by people, give them time and let them get on with it. Look at the United side on the day – there have been plenty of changes there. But then all of a sudden they'll get it right – the right blend, the right balance – and then they'll just go from strength to strength. United have proved this, but you have to let the manager get his ideas over.'

In his normal modest, unassuming manner Ian Brightwell chose this entire team performance as his idea of Blue Heaven. No one could have blamed him in the slightest if he had chosen the return derby at Old Trafford that season. Clayton Blackmore had given United a second-half lead with a diving header at the Stretford End. Five minutes later City equalised in spectacular style. Mark Ward laid the ball back in from the right-wing where Brightwell (according to him) 'just closed his eyes and wellied it.' From about 25 yards the ball flew from his left foot into the top corner of the net. This is undoubtedly Ian Brightwell's most personal memory from more than 11 years at Maine Road.

One of the big movies on show during the summer and autumn of 1989 was Kevin Costner's *Field of Dreams*, a baseball story set on a farm in Iowa. As far as Ian Brightwell is concerned, his 'field of dreams' was a football pitch in Moss Side, Manchester on 23 September 1989.

Saturday, 23 September 1989

Football League Division One at Maine Road

Manchester City	5	(Oldfield 2, Morley, Bishop, Hinchcliffe)
Manchester United	1	(Hughes)

MANCHESTER CITY	v.	MANCHESTER UNITED
Paul Cooper	1	Jim Leighton
Gary Fleming	2	Viv Anderson
Andy Hinchcliffe	3	Mal Donaghy
Ian Bishop	4	Mike Duxbury
Brian Gayle	5	Mike Phelan
Steve Redmond	6	Gary Pallister
David White	7	Russell Beardsmore
Trevor Morley	8	Paul Ince
David Oldfield	9	Brian McClair
Ian Brightwell	10	Mark Hughes
*Paul Lake	11	Danny Wallace
*Jason Beckford	SUB	Lee Sharpe
Gary Megson	SUB	Clayton Blackmore

Attendance: 43,246

3

GLYN PARDOE

City v. West Bromwich Albion
Football League Cup final at Wembley Stadium, 7 March 1970

A crowd of 21,941 saw City beaten 4–1 by Birmingham City at Maine Road on 11 April 1962. Making his debut for the Blues that day was Glyn Pardoe. He was just 15 years, 314 days old. On 17 March 1970 Pardoe was still in City's first team as they met West Bromwich Albion in the League Cup final at Wembley. The events of that day make the game the obvious choice for his idea of Blue Heaven.

He recalls: 'The FA Cup final is the one game that every professional player wants to play in, that's the game with all the glamour. Having said that however, scoring the winning goal in a League Cup final makes that a bit more special for me.'

The 1970 League Cup tournament was the first time all 92 clubs had taken part, a fact that was news to Glyn Pardoe: 'I didn't know that, but in all honesty facts and figures don't really mean that much when you're a player. You train hard in the week and play hard at weekends. As long as the team does well nobody even minded who scored. It was just a job really. Mind you, it was a good one!'

Glyn casts his mind back to events three days prior to that Wembley triumph 26 years ago: 'On the Wednesday night we played Academica Coimbra in a European Cup Winners' Cup tie in

Portugal. We flew to Portugal on the Monday and we had sun every day – the temperature was about 72–73 degrees. Theirs was a largely student side who played all in black and the pitch was bone-hard. We played the game (we drew nil-nil) and the plan was to fly back into London on the Thursday.'

He continues: 'We couldn't get into London – I remember this very clearly. The airport was snowed up and there was also a fireman's strike, so we had to land in Birmingham. We drove down to London and I remember all the side had a big fry-up breakfast in the early hours of the morning at the hotel.

'Joe went to see the Wembley pitch and told us it was awful – just like a cabbage patch. This was another reason the game was so special for me. We'd gone from the bone-hard surface in Portugal to this really heavy mud. You couldn't get much more of a difference in playing conditions.' (The pitch had been ruined recently by the staging of the Horse of the Year show, and during the week prior to the game, had been covered by snow and then by 20 tons of straw.) 'I suppose the preparations were not ideal for a Wembley Cup final, but they certainly meant that we were not left hanging around for a couple of days, trying to kill time.' During this limited preparation time, the team did manage a cinema trip to watch *Butch Cassidy and the Sundance Kid* and also managed to injure Harry Godwin in a five-a-side game.

City were knocked out of the previous year's League Cup by a solitary goal at Blackpool. The 1969–70 campaign began again at the Lancashire seaside – this time at Southport – where Alan Oakes, Colin Bell and Francis Lee scored the goals in a comfortable 3–0 win.

Much sterner opposition followed in the third round in the shape of Bill Shankly's Liverpool. Again City scored three goals (although they did concede two), with Mike Doyle, Neil Young and Ian Bowyer taking the goal-scoring honours this time.

On 15 October the blue half of Merseyside arrived at Maine Road for a fourth round tie. So intense was manager Harry Catterick's desire to win the First Division title that it was a much depleted Everton side (without Alan Ball and several other experienced first-teamers) which succumbed to a goal by Colin Bell and a Francis Lee penalty. Francis Lee said at the time: 'It was no contest really – Southport gave us more trouble!' Catterick's single-mindedness bore fruit at the end of the season when Everton won the title by nine points from second-placed Leeds United. They lost just five league games all term.

Another home tie in round five brought Queen's Park Rangers and the flamboyant Rodney Marsh to Maine Road. Two goals from Colin Bell and one from Mike Summerbee won the game 3–0, although it was a game in which City were strongly criticised for 'easing up'. This victory set up a tremendous two-legged semi-final against Manchester United.

A crowd of 55,799 packed into Maine Road on the night of Wednesday 3 December for the first leg. Just over a fortnight earlier City had beaten United 4–0 at Maine Road in a league game, but this semi-final proved a much closer affair. The return from injury of Nobby Stiles made a big difference to the Reds, although it was Colin Bell's fifth League Cup goal of the season which gave City the advantage at half-time. Bobby Charlton equalised in the second half before a last-minute penalty gave the Blues a priceless edge to take to Old Trafford for the second leg.

Francis Lee claims he was fouled by United's Ian Ure just as he was about to shoot (Ian Ure – and every other Red – claims he dived) and the much angered George Best received a booking and a four-week ban for knocking the ball out of the referee's hands. Needless to say the present goalkeeping coach was beaten by the present chairman's penalty kick – although he did guess the right way. More controversy and a bigger crowd – 63,418 – were to follow in the return leg two weeks later. An injury to Colin Bell meant the versatile David Connor would be City's only change, whereas United surprised everyone by replacing the in-form Brian Kidd with Denis Law, who was still not fully fit after a series of injuries. Mike Doyle was so confident of victory that he offered to buy all the United players dinner if City failed to win through to Wembley.

Doyle's money seemed safe (although it was never in any real danger, especially in those days) when Ian Bowyer's early goal put the Blues 1–0 up on the night and 3–1 up on aggregate. Paul Edwards levelled the score by half-time before Denis Law (a pity Kidd wasn't playing!) gave United the lead, and with it renewed confidence that perhaps it could still be the Reds and not the Blues marching down Wembley Way in three months' time.

In the dying minutes City were awarded a free-kick just outside United's Stretford End penalty area. A cramp-suffering Francis Lee blasted the ball through the Reds' wall and watched Alex Stepney make a parrying save. Mike Summerbee was first to react and before Stepney could recover the game was level at 2–2. Neither Lee nor Stepney had noticed the referee's raised arm indicating an indirect free-kick. If Stepney had let the ball in directly from the kick the goal would not have stood. However his goalkeeping instincts – coupled with the fact that he had been busy lining up his wall – forced him to make the save.

The cynics said that City had made it through to Wembley by way of a dubious penalty and a controversial free-kick. City fans knew the real reason. This was a great side who played open, attacking football and didn't know the meaning of defeat.

For the bulk of that 1969–70 season (and the three previous ones), Glyn Pardoe wore the number three shirt and played in an orthodox left-back position. The arrival of then record signing Arthur Mann in November 1968 moved Pardoe first to right-back (as cover for the injured Tony Book), and latterly for a time into midfield. He had worn the number seven shirt in Portugal and would be number 11 at Wembley. Did these changes bother him? 'No, not at all, just so long as I was playing I didn't mind. I was quite used to it. As a kid I'd played centre-half, midfield, both full-backs – I played everywhere. I started off with City as centre-forward!

'At one time I used to play centre-half for the school team, inside-forward for Mid-Cheshire and centre-forward for Cheshire. It really made no difference to me. Although I settled in at left-back I had no real preference for any position. I could have settled in anywhere.' After a leisurely noon-time walk, City went into their match-day team-talk at one-thirty. They made just one change from the side that drew in Portugal. In a perhaps surprise move, classy striker Neil Young (a Wembley winner less than 12 months previously) was replaced by defender George Heslop as the Blues adopted a 4–3–3 formation.

Because of the growing maturity of Tommy Booth, Heslop had played less than 20 league games since being a regular member of the Championship side of two seasons earlier. At one stage he had looked as though he might have been on the move to Middlesbrough, but he was brought in specifically for this game by Malcolm Allison to counter the threat of Albion's England striker Jeff Astle. (This is the same Jeff Astle who nowadays sings so beautifully in a variety of bizarre outfits on television's *Fantasy Football League*.)

Again the critics were out, declaring, 'City can't possibly win with such a defensive line-up.' With six minutes gone it looked like they could be right. Asa Hartford's through ball for Astle was turned behind for a corner by City skipper Tony Book. The corner was cleared first by Corrigan's fist and then by Doyle's head out to the left wing where Albion full-back Ray Wilson hoisted a high cross back into the Blues' penalty area. The ball was missed by Heslop and the nervous 21-year old goalkeeper Corrigan. It was met by Jeff Astle's forehead and the black and red stripes were a goal down. It was Astle's 24th goal of a season that would see him finish top scorer in Division One.

Glyn Pardoe recalls: 'Strangely enough from that moment on we hammered them – but we just could not get a goal.' Both press and players would later comment that the goal was more of a boost to City than it was to Albion.

Despite the remaining largely one-sided 40 or so minutes, City went in at half-time still with a one goal deficit. Francis Lee, having one of his best ever games for the Blues under the watchful eye of England manager Sir Alf Ramsey, remembers the ratio of attacks 'being something like ten to one in our favour'. Lee himself had a spectacular header turned over by Osborne and provided a wicked cross-shot which Mike Summerbee was unable to convert, owing to a desperate tackle on the line by centre-half John Talbot. West Bromwich Albion seemed largely unconcerned about all this pressure: they opened the champagne bottles during the half-time break!

Was it going to be one of those days – players and supporters know the kind – when no matter what City did, they would never get the equaliser? Everyone in the City camp was still 110 per cent confident and remained convinced that it was just a matter of time. Colin Suggett missed a glorious opportunity to make it 2–0 for Albion before the equaliser finally arrived in the 65th minute. Colin Bell was unable to make proper contact with Glyn Pardoe's glancing header and the ball went behind for a corner. Before the corner could be taken, trainer Dave Ewing came on to attend to the injured Mike Summerbee.

Glyn Pardoe takes up the story: 'We won a corner on the right wing and I took it. Mike Summerbee flicked it up, Colin Bell back-headed it and Mike Doyle rammed it in at the far post. I remember that moment as plain as anything. Doyley from about eight yards with his right foot.'

That flick would be Summerbee's last kick of the game. He was shortly to leave the field and was later diagnosed as having a hairline fracture of the left leg. His replacement was the 17 year-old Ian Bowyer, who himself was to receive certain discomfort to accompany his winners' medal. A blow to the head caused mild concussion and several stitches were required in an ankle wound.

The score remained 1–1 at full-time, which meant another gruelling 30 minutes' play on that heavy, mud-laden surface. After a hard-fought European tie three days earlier and the events of the previous 90 minutes, surely City had to be tired?

Not so, as Pardoe recalls today: 'I don't think you feel tiredness the same when you're on top. We were running the show and when that's the case you just don't notice it.

'I was playing against Asa Hartford; he was absolutely shattered and was substituted. We'd just run him into the ground. When you're on the field and on top you just sense it. I don't know what it is but you can just tell the signs. We never looked tired. We just kept going forward and the more you go forward the more it raises you.

'We were a very fit side with a great team spirit. Nobody ever gave up. We used to have some really open, heated discussions at half-time – especially if we were getting beat or one particular player was causing us trouble. Everybody would pull together. We were just like a family; I suppose we still are today.'

In the first period of extra-time Albion's substitute Dick Krzywicki rounded Joe Corrigan only to see his shot hit the side netting. It proved to be their last chance to win the game. After 112 minutes, City finally managed to score that all elusive second goal.

'I remember Franny picking the ball up on the right,' recalls Glyn today, 'and both Colin and I ran towards the near post. Franny chipped the ball up for Colin who then back-headed it into the box. I managed to get to the ball before both the keeper and Doug Fraser and hooked it into the net. Then they couldn't catch me!

'Everyone on the side thought it was going to come. We should have won the game during 90 minutes. Malcolm said to us during the break just to give Franny the ball – he was having such a good game

– and to keep on doing what we had been doing. He told us the break would come, and sure enough it did.'

City were the first Lancashire side (as they were then in the days prior to the many governmental changes) to lift the League Cup, and the first side ever to win the FA Cup and League Cup in successive seasons. There was also another first on that victorious day back in March 1970. Glyn Pardoe scored his first goal of the season. He had had a hand in the first goal, and then scored the winner shortly after he had seen another of his shots go inches over the bar.

His wife Pat, nearly seven months pregnant at the time, was in the stand but, according to Glyn, was not really watching the game. 'If it hadn't been for me she probably wouldn't have been a football fan. She didn't know it was me who'd scored. I think she was talking – like they do – and when everyone jumped up she asked who'd scored. I think it was Tony Book's wife Sylvia who told her.' Fortunately the shock of Glyn scoring had no ill effects on Pat and their daughter Vanessa was born in June.

One other incident makes this day even more special for Glyn Pardoe: 'About four days after the game, we'd finished training and were in the changing-rooms. Malcolm calls me over and says "Here you are, this is for you." It was the match ball signed by all the players. It was a great gesture. I've still got it at home, it's a bit old and decrepit but I'll always keep it.' The amount of attacking in the Wembley game bore a sharp contrast to the game in Coimbra. 'That was a very dour game with no more than three chances all night. They were very defensive and we, as the away side, were also trying to play it tight.' (This was, of course, a very rare strategy for City sides of the era.) 'Even the return leg at Maine Road was a struggle and we had to wait until extra-time for Tony Towers's winner.

'When West Brom scored we thought, "Bloody hell, we're losing here, we'd better do something." In a strange way that goal did us the world of good.' An extremely hard, physical game was over, and it meant City would be back in Europe the following year even if they didn't win the European Cup Winners' Cup. This, of course, was accomplished less than two months later when they triumphed over Polish side Gornik Zabrze in a rain-sodden Prater Stadium in Vienna. This success meant City were the first English side ever to win both a domestic and European trophy in the same season. 1970: a great year for firsts.

After the celebratory party at their London hotel with their wives – 'We'd had so much success that the wives knew each other almost as well as the players' – the team returned to Manchester on the Sunday. Here they were greeted by snow and sleet as well as 6,000 jubilant fans (including the author) in Albert Square. Only George Heslop, who'd justified his selection with a fine performance, was missing. He'd returned on the Saturday night to be with his wife, who was expecting their third baby.

City had nine league games left after that Wembley success. Of these they lost five – although they did manage a 2–1 win at Old Trafford – and finished the season in tenth place. These defeats included a 5–1 home thrashing by West Ham United in a game played in mud-bath conditions and memorable only for Ronnie Boyce's goal from the halfway line following Joe Corrigan's clearance.

The following season, 1970–71, saw Glyn Pardoe reverting to his regular left-back position. He played in all except one of the first 19 league games that season before the 12 December derby clash with United at Old Trafford.

City led 1–0 thanks to a 15th minute headed goal by Mike Doyle. Eight minutes later Glyn Pardoe suffered a horrendous broken leg which kept him out of the game for nearly two years. It was by no means a clean break: 'Oh no, it was a shocker – the tibia and the fibula. The leg was just hanging off. It was a real mess. The surgeon who repaired it for me, Norman Shaw, did a fantastic job on it. At one point it was touch and go as to whether or not the leg would have to be amputated.'

Pardoe continues: 'I think Sidney Rose came up from London to have a look at it. The arteries were trapped and he freed them before Mr Shaw put the leg back together.'

How had the injury occurred? 'I was just about to clear the ball when Besty jumped in at me. The positioning of my leg at exactly that moment meant it was impossible to deflect the blow and his studs just went clean through my right leg. It completely smashed the tibia and fibula.'

Pardoe was stretchered off the field and immediately rushed to hospital by ambulance. After consultation with the linesman, Best was booked. He appealed against the decision. Television evidence (by all accounts nowhere near the clarity of today's broadcasts) and a letter from Pardoe himself supported his plea and the booking was removed from his record. To say Best had got off lightly would certainly be an understatement – just ask any of Pardoe's team-mates.

City eventually won the game 4–1, thanks largely to a Francis Lee hat-trick, the only one scored by a First Division player away from home all season. As with Colin Bell nearly five years later, the severity of the injury took the edge off an otherwise great night for the Blues.

More than 25 years after the incident, Pardoe is now quite philosophical about the whole affair: 'After a while the leg wasn't healing as the doctors wished so I had to have a bone graft. I had about 15 inches of bone chipped out of my back and put into the leg.

'The only slight problem now is that the right foot is not as flexible as the left but I can live with that quite easily. If I'd been playing somewhere else at the time, who knows? I'd have probably lost the leg. Fortunately for me I had the right people there at the right time who were prepared to give me a chance. I was on the operating table for about four an a half hours – if I hadn't been so strong and fit I would probably have died.'

By sheer coincidence Glyn was reminded of his injury just weeks before I spoke to him: 'I was doing some Christmas shopping with Pat in town, walking towardsthe Arndale Centre. A complete stranger walked up to me and said "You're Glyn Pardoe aren't you?" I said "Yes I am." He said "Do you know what day it is?" I replied that it was the 12 December, to which he answered "Yes, the 25th anniversary of your injury!"

'It's very rare I go to town nowadays, so the chances of bumping into that man – who knew the significance of the date – on that particular day must be millions to one. I just couldn't believe it!'

The tragic incident at Old Trafford began a terrible run of injuries. Summerbee, Doyle, Booth, Book, Bell, Lee, and Pardoe's cousin Alan Oakes would later follow, and it was no surprise when – despite the valiant efforts of City's youngsters – the European Cup Winners' Cup was surrendered to Chelsea in the semi-final. Following Pardoe's injury City won just three of their remaining 23 league games and ended a disappointing season in 11th place. It was the first time in four years the Blues had failed to win a major prize. Pardoe returned to first team duties on 4 November 1972 in a 4–0 victory over Derby County at Maine Road. His leg had still not healed properly. 'It was okay at the sides – the bones had knitted together – but in the middle there was still a slight gap. The specialists said it was strong enough and would hold, and sure enough it did. Having done so much for me already, I wasn't going to question their decision.'

He played a further 43 league games before retiring on 30 April 1976. At the end of that season the Blues toured the Far East, playing the national sides of both Japan and South Korea. 'I went along with the party,' Glyn remembers, 'just to help out and for emergency cover. I ended up playing the last two games, both against South Korea, and both times we won 3–0.' The second game, on 3 June, was the last time Glyn Pardoe wore the famous sky blue shirt. It was also the last time he would run out onto the pitch and re-tie his boot laces before kick-off – a pre-match ritual he had practised since schoolboy days. His playing career of 374 (+2) senior appearances, stretching back 14 years, was over. To this day he is still the youngest player ever to play in City's first team and it seems highly unlikely that anyone will remove him from his place in the record books.

On his retirement (which incidentally was brought forward because of injuries to his left knee as opposed to his right one), Pardoe began coaching duties at Maine Road. 'I just fell into it really. Because I'd had these knee problems I wasn't playing every game and so I began to help out with the training. I had some free time after the treatment I was receiving and then Tony Book asked me to do a bit of scouting as well. It just sort of grew. In the end I was working full-time with the youth and reserve sides. I did it for 16 years before Peter Reid got the big brush out in 1992.'

After 31 years of loyal service, Glyn Pardoe was no longer employed by Manchester City Football Club. How did he feel? 'Not so good! I took about 12 months off – just relaxed and tried to sort myself out. Eventually I got a job with Barclays Bank at their computer centre in Knutsford. I work on the reception area. It's interesting work and I enjoy it. I've been there more than three years now.'

He still lives in the Cheshire village of Davenham where he lived when he was playing. Does he see anything of his cousin? 'All the time. He lives about half a mile from me, but I have to say I don't see many games. I've got a completely different lifestyle. When I was playing or coaching it was six, sometimes seven days a week with City.

'Now I work three days, three nights and get the next three days off. I see all my family and manage to play some golf. Mind you, I still look for City's results first. It'll always be my club. I was fortunate enough to have played in some great sides there and in all honesty I wouldn't swap my playing days for those of today – even though the money is a bit different!'

Saturday, 7 March 1970

Football League Cup final at Wembley Stadium

| Manchester City | 2 | (Doyle, Pardoe) |
| West Bromwich Albion | 1 | (Astle) |

MANCHESTER CITY   v. WEST BROMWICH ALBION

Joe Corrigan	1	John Osborne
Tony Book	2	Doug Fraser
Arthur Mann	3	Ray Wilson
Mike Doyle	4	Tony Brown
Tommy Booth	5	John Talbut
Alan Oakes	6	John Kaye
George Heslop	7	Len Cantello
Colin Bell	8	Colin Suggett
*Mike Summerbee	9	Jeff Astle
Francis Lee	10	Asa Hartford*
Glyn Pardoe	11	Bobby Hope
*Ian Bowyer	SUB	Dick Krzywicki*

Attendance: 97,963

4

KEN BARNES

City v. Birmingham City
FA Cup final at Wembley Stadium, 5 May 1956

Ken 'Beaky' Barnes was the club joker at Maine Road during the 1950s, and described as 'eager', 'perceptive' and 'the perfect wing-half'. He was born within sight of Birmingham City's St Andrew's ground on 16 March 1929. As a schoolboy he had played for their Colts side, but it was whilst serving with the RAF that he really began to get noticed.

Bolton Wanderers were one club who noticed, but they were told that the RAF would have first refusal on Barnes, both as an aircraftsman and as a footballer. Bolton were quite prepared to wait until his demob, such was their keenness to sign him.

Barnes recalls: 'Then one day I guested for Stafford Rangers who were playing in the Birmingham Combination.' (Barnes was stationed in Stafford during his National Service.) 'When demob came, for some unknown reason, I signed professional for Stafford. I think the main reason was simple – I just liked it there.'

His dad was less than amused: 'He said to me, "What've you done that for? How many opportunities do you want to become a professional footballer?" I said: "But I am." He said "Yes, but with Stafford Rangers!"'

In May 1950 Ken Barnes arrived at Maine Road – from Stafford

Rangers – but things could have been very different. 'There were several clubs interested in me – West Bromwich Albion, Sheffield Wednesday and Birmingham City as well as Manchester City. For some reason – I don't know what it was – I chose City!'

When asked to describe his idea of Blue Heaven, Barnes replied, 'It's a very difficult decision. There were so many to choose from.'

He continued: 'I remember the three wins we had over United – 5–0 at Old Trafford, 3–2 at Maine Road and 2–0 in the FA Cup. We beat them three times that year, 1954–55. Then there's the semi-finals, the finals, the one with virtually ten men against Newcastle, and I also remember my first goal for City, against Derby County.'

He recalls a particular incident during that 5–0 game, although he doesn't choose it as his most memorable match. 'I remember they pushed Duncan Edwards up to inside-left to add a bit of punch to the attack. I seem to recall Dennis Viollet was injured. Young Duncan was a Midlander like myself, he was from Dudley and I was from Birmingham. At one point I said to him, "What the hell are you doing? You're no bloody good up here, get back there!"' Sheepishly, Edwards returned to his defensive position.

The name of Ken Barnes appears in the footballing record books for an unusual goalscoring feat: 'I got a hat-trick of penalties against Everton in December 1957. The first one I put low to the goalkeeper's left, this was the way I usually put them. The second one I put in the opposite corner, the goalkeeper's right. When the third one came along I was stumped. I looked at Everton's goalie George Dunlop and said, "You've no chance with this one – I don't know where it's going myself!" In the entire history of the Football League only two other players have achieved this remarkable feat. Billy 'The Goal Machine' Walker did it for Aston Villa against Bradford in November 1921, and Charlie Mitten equalled it in March 1950 when playing for Manchester United against Aston Villa.

Barnes was captain of the City side which led Luton 6–2 in the famous abandoned FA Cup tie back in January 1961. What is not widely known is the fact that in the rearranged game four days later, Barnes pulled a hamstring muscle, forcing him to play for 80 minutes as a 'limping right-winger'. 'I stayed on just to be a nuisance,' he says. In those pre-substitute days this is perhaps one of the reasons the Blues lost the game 2–1.

Eventually Ken decided on his most memorable game: 'I suppose winning the FA Cup final has to be the most important one, especially as we'd been there the year before and lost.' This is, of course, the 1956 FA Cup final – Manchester City 3 Birmingham City 1 – for ever remembered as 'Trautmann's Match'.

It had been a marvellous season for Birmingham. Twelve months earlier they had won promotion from the Second Division and, such was the calibre of their football, they finished the 1955–56 season in sixth place. They had been as high as third at one stage.

Their route to Wembley had not been easy, they played every one of their games away from home. A total of 18 goals were scored (including seven against Torquay United), whilst only two were conceded. Much credit for this defensive record went to England's goalkeeper Gil Merrick and his international full-back colleague Jeff Hall. (Hall was to die tragically less than three years after this game, stricken by polio. He was just 29.)

City's road to Wembley took in a variety of weather conditions. The third round home tie with Blackpool was abandoned due to fog with the score at 1–1. City won the rearranged match 2–1, thanks to goals from Bobby Johnstone and Jack Dyson. They travelled to Southend in the fourth round where Joe Hayes's solitary goal won the match in quagmire conditions. This was the famous 'Cockleshell' game.

More than 70,000 spectators packed into Maine Road for the fifth round clash with Liverpool on 18 February. A goalless draw preceded the Blues' 2–1 replay victory the following week, Hayes and Dyson winning the game for City despite Billy Liddell's 'equaliser' after the final whistle.

Seventy-six thousand people saw Everton beaten by the same scoreline at Maine Road in the quarter-final, Johnstone keeping Hayes company on the scoresheet this time. Johnstone's third FA Cup goal of the season was enough to beat Tottenham in the semi-final at Villa Park, and the Blues were back at Wembley, just as captain Roy Paul had promised after the disappointment of losing to Newcastle the previous year.

Although Barnes joined City in 1950, it took him until the start of the 1954–55 season to break through into the first team. 'When I arrived,' he recalls, 'I think there was something like nine wing-halves at the club.'

His time spent in the reserve sides was not wasted, however. Barnes became a key figure in the implementation of a new style of play at Maine Road – one that would revolutionise English football. This style later became known as 'The Revie Plan', and it would be this method that would bring the FA Cup back to Maine Road for the first time in 22 years.

'It was actually Johnny Williamson and myself who tried it in the reserve team. It worked quite well, and we went 20-odd games without defeat. Manager Les McDowall was then asked why we didn't try it in the first team. He was reluctant at first and said, "No, we'll never get away with it." Anyway in the finish he deemed to try it, and we played it in the first game of the 1954–55 season.' This was away at Preston and the Blues lost 5–0.

Barnes is quick to point out: 'I wasn't in the side, mind you. They tried the reserve team plan with the first team players. Don Revie said to McDowall, "We need Ken Barnes in this team. He's the man who'll link it all together." Anyway, I was in for the next game (a 5–2 victory against Sheffield United), and I played in every game except one for the rest of the season.'

Ken also remembers TV commentator Kenneth Wolstenholme writing for a newspaper that season. 'I've been to see the Magyars from Maine Road,' he said, referring of course to the famous 1953 Hungarian side which had triumphed at Wembley against the hitherto invincible England team.

Ken Barnes confirms the opinions of his team-mate Roy Clarke: 'It wasn't something that was coached. It was just intuition. Every player knew what every other was supposed to do. Over the years I've seen various coaching methods spoil too many things, too many players. I'm a great believer in trainers, not coaches. A coach is a charabanc we used to go to the seaside in!'

He continues: 'It wasn't a great plan really; it was just something a bit different. All teams then used to play with a big, robust centre-forward. Players like Bolton's Nat Lofthouse and Trevor Ford of Aston Villa and Sunderland. Wingers would knock crosses in for them, inside-forwards would put through passes into the box.

'Our centre-forward played off the centre-half. This confused their defence. Up until that point they'd been used to a one-on-one situation with the centre-forward. Now they were looking around for

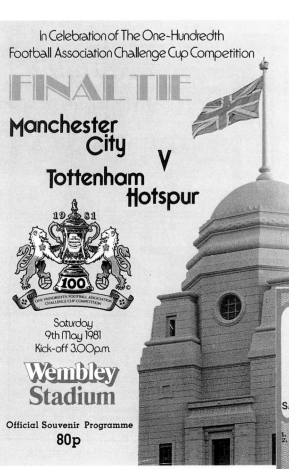

In Celebration of The One-Hundredth
Football Association Challenge Cup Competition

FINAL TIE

Manchester City
v
Tottenham Hotspur

1981

ONE HUNDREDTH FOOTBALL ASSOCIATION
CHALLENGE CUP COMPETITION

Saturday
9th May 1981
Kick-off 3.00 p.m.

Wembley Stadium

Official Souvenir Programme

80p

(LEFT AND BELOW) Joe's idea of Blue Heaven: City v. Spurs in the 1981 FA Cup final

(BOTTOM) Joe Corrigan points proudly to the 'Save of the Season' painting which hangs on his living-room wall

THE EMPIRE STADIUM, WEMBLEY

No ticket genuine unless it carries
a Lion's Head watermark below

1981

ONE HUNDREDTH FOOTBALL ASSOCIATION
CHALLENGE CUP COMPETITION

FINAL TIE

SATURDAY, MAY, 9 1981

KICK-OFF 3.00 p.m.
YOU ARE ADVISED TO TAKE UP
YOUR POSITION BY 2.30 p.m.

1. This ticket is not transferable.
2. This counterfoil must be retained for at least 6 months.

J.S. Lott CHAIRMAN
WEMBLEY STADIUM LTD

NORTH STAND SEAT

£16.00

TO BE RETAINED   SEE PLAN AND CONDITIONS ON BACK

TURNSTILES
E
ENTRANCE
84
ROW
14
SEAT
19

(LEFT) Ian Brightwell, pictured at the Platt Lane training complex

(BELOW) Ian's Blue Heaven: City v. United in September 1989

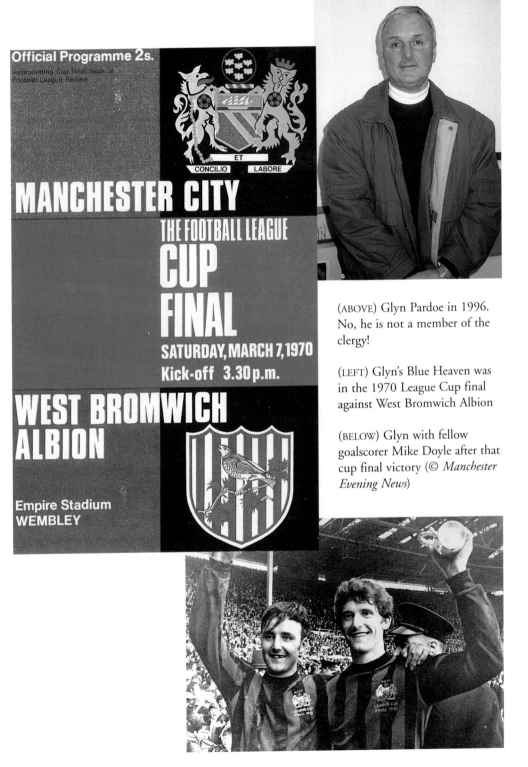

(ABOVE) Glyn Pardoe in 1996. No, he is not a member of the clergy!

(LEFT) Glyn's Blue Heaven was in the 1970 League Cup final against West Bromwich Albion

(BELOW) Glyn with fellow goalscorer Mike Doyle after that cup final victory (© *Manchester Evening News*)

(LEFT) Ken Barnes shows off the shirt he wore in the 1956 FA Cup final

(BELOW) Ken follows team-mates Roy Clarke and captain Roy Paul down the Wembley steps after the match (© *Manchester Evening News*)

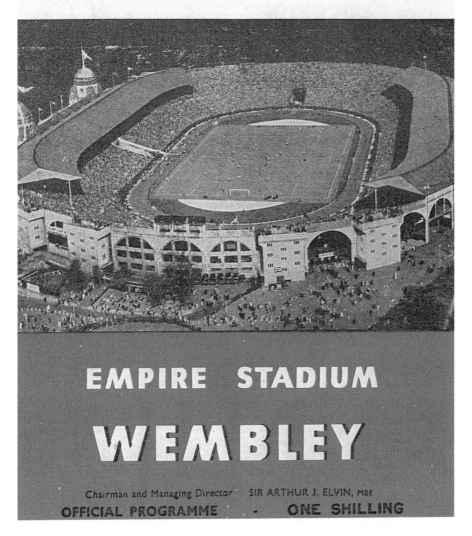

THE FOOTBALL ASSOCIATION CHALLENGE CUP COMPETITION

FINAL TIE
BIRMINGHAM CITY
v
MANCHESTER CITY

SATURDAY, MAY 5th, 1956   KICK-OFF 3 pm

EMPIRE STADIUM

WEMBLEY

Chairman and Managing Director   SIR ARTHUR J. ELVIN, MBE

OFFICIAL PROGRAMME   -   ONE SHILLING

(FAR LEFT AND ABOVE) City v. Birmingham City: Ken's Blue Heaven

MANCHESTER
CITY

versus

EVERTON

SATURDAY
22nd MARCH
1969 at 3.0 p.m.
Official
Souvenir
Programme
TWO SHILLINGS

(LEFT AND BELOW RIGHT) Tommy Booth's idea of Blue Heaven: City v. Everton in the 1969 FA Cup semi-final

(OPPOSITE) Tommy proudly exhibits his FA Cup and European Cup Winners' Cup medals

(BELOW) The great City trio of Lee, Bell and Summerbee congratulate the young Tommy Booth after his winning goal at Villa Park (© *Manchester Evening News*)

ASTON VILLA FOOTBALL CLUB LTD.

VILLA PARK - BIRMINGHAM   № 18679

F.A. CHALLENGE CUP - SEMI-FINAL

SATURDAY, 22nd MARCH, 1969 - KICK-OFF 3.00 P.M.

Manchester City v Everton
Terrace Standing 7/6

Entrance WITTON

Block   X   LANE

Secretary

Aston Villa F.C. Ltd.

If postponed, this ticket will be valid for the date on which the match is re-arranged.
This ticket is issued subject to the By-laws and Regulations of the Football Association.

(ABOVE) Paul Power pictured in the offices of the Professional Footballers' Association

(RIGHT) Paul's Blue Heaven: City v. Ipswich in the 1981 FA Cup semi-final

FA Cup Semi Final

MANCHESTER CITY
IPSWICH TOWN

SATURDAY 11th APRIL 1981
AT VILLA PARK · BIRMINGHAM
OFFICIAL PROGRAMME 50p

him, they didn't know where he was. And they were reluctant to leave their position to go and look for him. It bewildered teams for a long time. It certainly bewildered Birmingham!'

City had travelled down the week prior to the game and spent ten days on the south coast at Eastbourne. Despite City's success with The Revie Plan, manager McDowall was still uncertain on the morning of the game as to whether or not to play it – and Revie.

'All that week we'd been discussing how to play and who to play,' recalls Barnes. 'Bobby Johnstone had a slight calf-strain and Don Revie had played only half the season.' (It has since been reported that McDowall and Revie had had various disagreements throughout the season. This meant that Revie had only played 21 league games and, so far, just one FA Cup tie. Whatever the reasons, six months after the final, Don Revie left Maine Road and moved to Sunderland.)

'I was adamant Don should play,' says Barnes. 'But McDowall was worried about us having too many footballers.' The manager's mind was made up for him just after midday when the unfortunate Billy Spurdle had to withdraw with an attack of boils. Don Revie was in.

Shortly before kick-off Barnes went into the toilets for 'a quick rinse and a fag'. 'Les McDowall came in,' he remembers, 'and says, "What the bloody hell are you doing?" I said, "What's the matter? I have one before every match. It's no different just because it's Wembley. I've got to steady my nerves and you know I always have a fag, whether you like it or not."'

Most players during Barnes's career smoked. 'But no one let anyone else know. I used to go into the toilets and light up and just sit down. Then, one by one, the players would come past. "Give us a drag, Ken," they'd say. After a few minutes my fag would be like a wet lettuce!'

Barnes also recalls another conversation with McDowall: 'He told me to keep an eye on their inside-left Peter Murphy to make sure he didn't score. I replied, "How can I watch him if I'm at the other end helping the attack?" I wanted to play my own game.'

Three minutes into the game City, looking very continental in their maroon and white striped shirts, were a goal up. The Revie Plan was in full swing. Revie out wide to Clarke, back to Revie, forward to Hayes and a left-foot shot into the corner.

Twelve minutes later Birmingham were level, inside-right Noel Kinsey's shot beating Trautmann before going into the net via a post. The scoreline remained the same until half-time.

During the break, Revie spoke to Barnes. 'He said to me, "Where've you been?" I replied, "You heard him, back in the dressing-room before we went out: make sure Murphy doesn't score." He was very explicit.' Revie's next comment was even more explicit: 'Bollocks to him – come on, let's go and bloody play!'

That's exactly what Barnes and City did. Second-half goals from Jack Dyson and Bobby Johnstone within the space of three minutes secured victory. Barnes remembers City playing so well that 'we could have won by four or five'.

'That little chat really changed the game,' he recalls. 'Coaches and managers today tell players this, that and the other but, at the end of the day, once you're on the pitch you have to sort things out for yourselves. I had a hand in the second goal when I laid the ball on for Jack Dyson. I doubt if I'd ever been in that position in the first half.'

The game had just 17 minutes left when the incident which would be remembered for all time occurred. A Birmingham attack through the centre of City's defence was thwarted by the courage and awareness of Bert Trautmann. Showing great bravery, he hurled himself at the feet of the on-rushing Peter Murphy. (Where was Ken Barnes?) Bert smothered the ball, but in doing so (and completely unknown to everyone at the time including himself) broke his neck. Such was Trautmann's courage that after being revived he continued the game, surviving not only another dive at a forward's feet (this time centre-forward Eddy Brown), but also a collision with team-mate Dave Ewing who was trying to protect him.

According to Ken Barnes, 'Bert didn't know the seriousness of his injury for about three or four weeks. We were fairly close pals and he would pick me up from my house in Burnage and take me to the ground. He had tests and X-rays and they found nothing.

'One day a radiologist friend of Bert's asked him if he could take a look at it. He was under the X-ray for about an hour, and photographed from all angles. Then he found it. I suppose it was something like a hairline fracture, that's why they'd all missed it. Who knows, it might have healed itself but it would have been dicey.'

Another problem for City that day was locating Roy Little's winner's medal. In all the excitement, Roy had rolled it up with his shirt and thrown it in the laundry basket!

After the game City's players and staff (including Trautmann with his unknown broken second vertebra), made their way to The Café Royal for a celebration banquet. Their meal was interrupted by a delivery of the *Manchester Evening News* Cup final edition, which was specially flown into London, two hours before any other newspaper would hit the newsstands.

The following day the victorious team left the train at Manchester's London Road station and boarded an open-topped, single-decked Fingland's bus for a procession through the streets to the Town Hall. On arrival they were met by the Lord Mayor, Alderman Tom Regan, who gave them a civic welcome before captain Roy Paul addressed the thousands of fans packed into Albert Square.

On Monday 7 May, the *Manchester Evening News* published a special Cup final souvenir. This contained nearly 30 photographs of both the game and the team's triumphant return. There are also some marvellous advertisements. C & A Modes Ltd promised 'a gay summer' in a matching dress and jacket for four guineas, whilst smoked haddock was 'only one and ten per pound' until 12 May. What happened to it after that, we shall never know!

In that same newspaper Eric Thornton (later the author of a fine book on City entitled *Meredith to Mercer and the FA Cup*) wrote the following article:

> When the festooned Cup special snorted its way to Manchester's London Road station this evening and the cheers of the crowd roared in greeting to Manchester City's Wembley heroes, it was 'the end of the road' for at least six personalities – manager Les McDowall, trainer Laurie Barnett, and Roy Paul, Bert Trautmann, Bill Leivers and Ken Barnes.
>
> Mr McDowall has completed his plan to put City back on the map. You'll remember, of course, they were a very mediocre outfit when he left Wrexham to take over the managership of a club he had once captained.
>
> It was hard going. But gradually he shaped the nucleus of a new team, moved them gradually up the league ladder, and then

built them into a fighting force. Twelve months ago it looked as if his dream of taking a winning team back home from Wembley was shattered. But shortly afterwards he said to me, 'I can't rid myself of the feeling that we'll be back again in quick time.'

And so we all say congratulations Leslie McDowall.

Mr Barnett includes a 1934 Cup winner's medal in his collection of soccer prizes. Yet once the club with which he won it had appointed him senior trainer, he thought only of one target – training a team to 'lift' the Cup. Last year it very nearly materialised. When it did not he merely mused afterwards on the quiet journey home, 'We'll have to start all over again and have another go.'

If you had the chance to see his face, as I had shortly after the players had trooped off the field, aglow with their success over Birmingham, there could not have been the slightest doubt in your mind about his happiness.

Roy Paul has never made any secret of his lifelong ambition. Having gained international honours at an early age he was always thinking of the thrill of possessing a Cup medal. I know he got one last May. But it was not the one he wanted. It was a loser's award.

That was why he kept saying to me all this winter that if Sam Cowan was capable of taking a City team to Wembley in successive years – as he did in 1933 and 1934 – and winning on the second occasion, he did not see any reason why he should not repeat the act.

What was his reaction on entering the dressing-room as captain of the winning team? First of all he gathered the signatures of all his City team-mates on the ball with which they had just beaten Birmingham. Then, easing open the outer door from the sacred precincts of the dressing-room to the outside world, Roy quietly passed the ball to his little son with these words: 'Never lose that son. It was the ball that won the Cup for your dad.'

Then he spent a delirious 20 minutes walking round and round the dressing-room in just a vest, making certain every one of his friends had had a drink from the Cup. Gradually he manoeuvred some of his friends from the Rhondda Valley into the dressing-room and anybody could have been forgiven for thinking they were really in Welsh Wales.

But Paul couldn't have cared less. It was his greatest moment.

Bert Trautmann had got his eyes on the target from the moment he signed for City from St Helens Town, the Lancashire Combination club. Above all there were two things in his young athletic life which were forever spotlighted ahead – playing for Germany and being presented with a Cup medal by Her Majesty the Queen.

It was a severe blow to his pride when Germany passed him over for the Wembley match with England. I took him to that game. It was his first visit to the famous stadium. I shall never forget that moment later when, on the night train home he said to me, 'If I live to be 100 I shall never stop hoping to play at Wembley.'

When City were through again to the final he said, 'Now I've been given the terrific honour of Footballer of the Year, so we have simply got to win that Cup.'

I will never forget helping trainer Barnett with a dressing-room massage to ease the pain in Trautmann's neck at the end of the Wembley triumph against Birmingham. He put both his great hands on my shoulders and said, 'By crikey, the pain stabs right through me . . .' There came a second's pause. Then he added, 'But it's worth it. I don't care if the pain's like a red-hot poker. I know I've got that Cup medal in my wallet.'

Bill Leivers, a very quiet fellow, badly wanted to play at Wembley. When he left Chesterfield to join Manchester City, some of his pals said, 'It will be hard making the grade.' Bill sensed, rightly or wrongly, that some of them thought he was stepping up into better class soccer without much chance of success. I remember how he was first introduced into the first team as a right full-back. It was not a very happy occasion.

So Mr Leivers stepped back into the reserves. But his ambitions didn't do that. He continued looking forward to the time when he could say to those Chesterfield doubters that he had played at Wembley and done well.

So you can well imagine how he felt after the final, especially as his performance at right full-back had been so polished. When I congratulated him he just said, 'Now the boys back home will know I've made the grade.'

Ken Barnes is a different character from the rest. Like his great friend Roy Little he's a born humourist – yet deep down this brilliant right half from Stafford has been nursing a dream for years.

Having been born just outside Birmingham City's headquarters at St Andrew's, he naturally wanted to show them what they had missed. Yet every time City played down there they seemed to take a thrashing. At least that was the way of things until the sixth round there last year when City triumphed and Ken was one of the heroes.

At the start of this season he said to me, 'I'd love to have a Wembley winner's medal to show everybody in Birmingham.' Now he's got it and if you'd spoken to him this weekend, as so many of his close friends did in the hotel, you'd have heard him reiterating this phrase: 'I just want to die. I'm so happy.'

So there you are. A bunch of great-hearted fellows who have 'reached the end of the road.'

'CITY – WE'RE PROUD OF YOU!' read another headline. It continued:

United share finest double for 50 years. Yes, we can realise it now, THE CUP'S OURS!

After the agony, the suspense and the tension of these past weeks, and then the super climax of the Wembley final itself, all Manchester can breathe freely again and revel in the title 'King Soccer City of Britain.'

That title is fully deserved. Manchester United played their part with a triumphant run in the League to carry off the Championship crown and to make sure of the first leg of this fabulous double. And then on Saturday, against all the odds, Manchester City battled to a magnificent 3–1 victory over Birmingham City in the FA Cup final.

And what a match. Surely those who saw it, either at the Wembley Stadium or on television, will never forget it. Truly it was the game of a lifetime. For Manchester City it was a double victory, for they also had to battle with the injury bogy which dogged them right up to zero hour. From Eastbourne where the team spent the last ten days training for the game came daily reports, each one telling of the casualties.

First Bobby Johnstone, key man in the attack, was doubtful with a strained muscle, then just as he was getting right came the news of full-back Bill Leivers. And on Friday – Wembley eve – down went Billy Spurdle with an attack of boils. Luckily Johnstone and Leivers recovered in time for the big game but poor Spurdle was forced to watch it from the stands.

Into the side came Don Revie, and with a limping Johnstone on the wing they took the field against the mighty Birmingham side. The story of the battle that followed is soccer history now, but it will be a long time before Manchester football fans forget it. City and United have achieved the greatest Cup and League feat for 50 years – since Liverpool and Everton won the League and Cup in 1906.

All this talk of doubles probably sounded marvellous 40 years ago. Somehow the magic word 'double' doesn't have the same ring to Blues followers in the 1990s!

Following Roy Paul's departure in 1957, Ken Barnes took over the captaincy at Maine Road. Over the next four years Barnes nurtured the talents of many aspiring youngsters including future managing director Colin Barlow and a small, thin Scot by the name of Denis Law. 'I taught him to drive his first car, and he still calls round nowadays for a cuppa!'

On 4 May 1961 Ken Barnes became player-manager of Wrexham. He had scored 19 times in 283 league and cup appearances since arriving from Stafford Rangers 11 years earlier. He was 32 when he moved to Wrexham, where he was to play 132 league games. He also gained promotion one year and just missed out again the next. All in all his time at Wrexham was reasonably successful, but differences of opinion with the chairman would bring about his departure in 1965. He then moved to Cheshire League side Witton Albion before a brief 'summer job' with Bangor.

In August 1970 Ken Barnes was asked by Joe Mercer to return to Maine Road as first team trainer. He continued these duties all through the period of turmoil when Joe moved to Coventry, right through to the enforced retirement of Johnny Hart.

When Ron Saunders came in as manager, Barnes thought his training days were numbered. 'He more or less ran all the training sessions. I was nothing more than a glorified ballboy and I told him I wasn't happy.' Fortunately for Ken, this time of unease coincided with the retirement of chief scout Harry Godwin and he was offered the position. 'I thought to myself that the scout's job is more secure than the trainer's – bearing in mind the changes when a new manager takes over.'

It was a secure job all right – he was scouting for City between 1974 and 1992. In May that year Ken Barnes lost his job, along with many others, during Peter Reid's backroom restructuring. During his time as chief scout he discovered more than 30 players who would go on to play either Premier League or First Division football. Admittedly some of these were with other clubs, but Steve Redmond, David White and Paul Lake are examples of those who made it at Maine Road.

In 1996 he's back scouting for his beloved City, albeit on a part-time basis. 'Francis asked me to come back in an advisory capacity. My first reaction was, "Are you the manager as well as the chairman? He might have his own people." Anyway, they had a meeting and fortunately I was invited back. I like to think I can offer them my experience and they know I'd do anything for the club.

'The atmosphere here today is marvellous. I've never known it so good; it is so homely and welcoming. I just wish more than anything that we could win something because, by God, everyone connected with the club deserves it.'

FA Cup final at Wembley Stadium

Manchester City	3	(Hayes, Dyson, Johnstone)
Birmingham City	1	(Kinsey)

MANCHESTER CITY	v.	BIRMINGHAM CITY
Bert Trautmann	1	Gil Merrick
Bill Leivers	2	Jeff Hall
Roy Little	3	Ken Green
Ken Barnes	4	John Newman
Dave Ewing	5	Trevor Smith
Roy Paul	6	Len Boyd
Bobby Johnstone	7	Gordon Astall
Joe Hayes	8	Noel Kinsey
Don Revie	9	Eddy Brown
Jack Dyson	10	Peter Murphy
Roy Clarke	11	Alex Govan

Attendance: 100,000

5

TOMMY BOOTH

City v. Everton
FA Cup semi-final at Villa Park, 22 March 1969

The late Harry Godwin, City's former chief scout responsible for providing the Blues with an array of young talent during the '60s and '70s, plays a part in a supposedly true story concerning the baby Tommy Booth. Tommy remembers: 'Harry used to drink in the same pub as my dad (incidentally also called Tommy): The Lion and Lamb on Victoria Avenue. For a few weeks either side of my birth my dad hadn't been out much and then one day he finally bumped into Harry.

'All right Tommy, what's she had then?' enquires Godwin.

'A boy', replies Booth senior.

'Right,' says Godwin, 'we'll get him signed up as soon as he's old enough and can wear boots.'

That same story is also reported in Peter Gardner's *Manchester City Football Book Number 3* (published in 1971) so there must be at least a grain of truth in it. Who cares if there isn't, anyway? It's still a good story. On 16 January 1965 City lost 2–1 to Swindon Town in a league game at Maine Road. Future Blues' favourite Mike Summerbee scored for Swindon that day in front of a crowd of just 8,015. To this day it is City's lowest attendance for a home game.

The 15 year-old Tommy Booth was one of the chosen (if that is the right word) few that day. He recalls: 'I was brought up supporting

City and was genuinely in the crowd that day. Mind you since then I've heard so many people say they were there too that there must have been in the region of 90,000 people there.' A similar thing could be said about the 1968 Championship decider at Newcastle.

At the time of that Swindon game Booth was playing regularly for both Middleton Boys and Manchester Catholic Boys. Then one day Harry Godwin invited him down to Maine Road for trials. 'It was fantastic,' remembers Booth today. 'I was just a fan and couldn't really believe it.' He played well enough to pass the test and joined the club as an amateur in September 1965.

'Later on Malcolm saw me play in a Sunday league game and asked Harry about the big lad playing up front. "He's already on the books," said Harry. Malcolm had another look at me and eventually asked me to sign apprentice professional forms.'

The wiser head of Tommy Booth senior played a key part in the next phase of Tommy junior's career. 'My dad wouldn't let me sign at first. He said – and probably rightly so – that there were lots of lads who signed up then never made it.'

All the time the young Booth was blossoming as a footballer he was serving an 18-month apprenticeship with the large east-Manchester engineering firm of Mather & Platt. It was this apprenticeship that Tommy senior wanted to see completed before allowing Tommy junior to take the plunge as a full-time footballer.

'Finish the 18 months and see what happens then,' remembers the younger Booth today. 'What a great time that was,' he quipped, his tongue planted firmly in his cheek. 'Every Tuesday and Thursday after work I used to make my way down to the training ground in Urmston, and then afterwards Harry Godwin would give me a lift home. When I was 17 City offered me a two-year full-time contract and my dad told me to take it.' Booth's debut appearance in City's first team came as a substitute in a League Cup tie at Huddersfield in September 1968. The following month he started a game for the first time as City drew 1–1 with Arsenal at Maine Road.

For 28 of the last 30 league games that season Tommy Booth kept George Heslop out of the side at the heart of the Blues' defence. He would also play in all seven City FA Cup ties that term, culminating in the 1–0 triumph over Leicester City at Wembley. Not surprisingly, therefore, Tommy's idea of Blue Heaven comes from a game played during that successful FA Cup campaign – the semi-final against Everton at Villa Park.

City had made their way to Villa Park having beaten Luton Town, Newcastle United (after a replay), Blackburn Rovers and Tottenham, and had the proud record of conceding just one goal along the way.

Booth's memories of the game were not just about the football itself: 'It was the build-up towards the game. I had to arrange all the tickets and coaches in order to get my dad and the rest of the family down for the game. As far as the team was concerned, our main discussion had been about Everton's three great midfield players: Howard Kendall, Alan Ball and Colin Harvey. These three England internationals made Everton possibly slight favourites on the day, but both sides on paper were evenly matched.'

Tommy's job that day was to mark Joe Royle, another Evertonian who would later have Maine Road connections. 'We had a game plan,' Booth told me. 'Joe and Malcolm decided to put Dave Connor on Alan Ball and he literally never gave him a kick. We were in control of the game most of the time although we didn't have many clear chances. Everton on the other hand had practically none.'

City played Francis Lee in the game despite him not being fully fit and refusing pain-killing injections prior to kick-off. Further problems would follow just 15 minutes into the game when Mike Doyle was carried off with an ankle injury following a collision with Joe Royle. At this point Joe Mercer and Malcolm Allison gambled and played the next quarter of an hour with just ten men, a repaired Doyle returning to the action on the half-hour.

As time went on the game looked more and more like a goalless draw, with a replay seeming inevitable. Booth remembers Neil Young breaking through in the dying moments: 'Youngie had a tremendous shot, as everyone knew, and when he hit it, it swung and dipped and went all over the place. It never used to go straight. Everton's goalkeeper at the time was Gordon West, and as he moved one way to stop Young's shot, the ball swerved the other and struck him on the shoulder. I'm sure he knew nothing about it – the ball just hit him and flew over for a corner.'

Tommy thought City's last chance had gone: 'We all thought, "That's it – a replay." Anyway, Youngie takes the corner and everyone was up in their area. The ball goes to the back post where Mike

Summerbee knocks it down and back across the goal. As it comes down – I remember Colin Bell being next to me – it just bounced nicely and I struck it as hard as I could with my left foot. The City fans behind the goal erupted.' The emotion and relief for Blues fans at that moment has obviously fogged their memories. Booth recalls, 'A lot of fans even today ask me if the best goal I ever scored was that header at Villa Park.'

Everton had very nearly got away with it, just like the infamous Kray twins who days before this game had been jailed for life at the Old Bailey. Tommy Booth senior – like many hundreds of fans on that day – had given up the game as a draw and left the ground before the final whistle. He never saw his son's greatest moment.

'The following day the goal was shown on television,' recalls Tommy junior, 'and he never saw it then either! Our house was full of reporters all desperate for interviews. We ended up buying a video years later so he could see it.'

Booth casts his mind back to the fine Everton side that played on that March day, some 27 years ago: 'Apart from those three great midfielders and big Joe Royle, they also had Johnny Morrisey on the wing and Brian Labone at the back. All in all they had a very good team, but on the day we just stifled them. We never gave them a chance to play – it was a fair result. We literally squeezed Everton in the middle of the park. We pushed them right back and never gave them an opportunity to attack us.' For City, David Connor had an outstanding game, and Booth rated him highly as an all-rounder, similar to Paul Madeley of Leeds United. Stories abound of the great City sides of the late '60s and early '70s never having team-talks let alone a game plan. 'There's the ball, there's the pitch, go out and play' is just one of these tales. Booth says: 'Yes, those stories were around for years about how we would just go out and play off the cuff. All right some players can do that, but you've got to have discipline in the team to know what to do. You can't just go out and chase everything. The really great players are told "We'll just let you do this", the likes of Best and Marsh, but within the structure of the team you must have players who know what to do.'

League champions in 1968, FA Cup finalists 12 months later – everyone in the country knew what a great side Manchester City was.

Tommy recounts a story which perhaps could only be told about

City: 'After the Everton game we were having some photographs taken in the dressing-room and Albert Alexander, the chairman, walks in. He said, "Well done, lads, we've made it to the final. Just think, with all the money we'll make, we can go out and buy some new players." Thanks very much!'

In that same dressing-room manager Joe Mercer (clutching an Allison-like cigar and champagne glass) told reporters, 'Now the tension is over we can go to Wembley and play football'. It was something that great side was always capable of doing.

City had travelled to Birmingham the day before the game and had stayed overnight in a Matlock hotel where they had their pre-match meal. The victorious side stopped off there on their way back as well. 'I was 18 at the time and I'd just scored the winner in the FA Cup semi-final. Well, you can imagine what happened. I got absolutely legless – I didn't know what day it was.

'Eventually the coach got the players back to Manchester. They put me in a taxi and sent me home to Langley. I remember falling out of the taxi – it was something like four or five in the morning – and everywhere there seemed to be red and black flags and banners. I didn't have a clue where I was.'

With a maternal 'Where have you been?' Tommy's mum helped him from the gutter and into the house where his dad undressed him and got him into bed. 'I was asleep for about two hours when my mum woke me up saying "You'd better get a quick shower; the press are waiting for you downstairs." When I got down I then realised what the banners were – "Well Done Tommy" – as far as the eye could see. The neighbours had been really busy! The press had all the kids in the street there wanting me to play football with them. So there I was, kicking and heading the ball, and smiling all the way through it. All the kids were shouting. I felt absolutely awful; like death warmed up.'

Tommy's condition was down to his more experienced team-mates the night before, although he does claim that they didn't mix his drinks. 'It was just the fact I wasn't used to it. I'd never really tasted champagne before. As time went on, though, I got more and more used to drinking with the lads. We had some good players in those days and some good drinkers as well, so it was a case of having to get used to it.'

City had won the championship in 1968 with a team of 11

Englishmen and a forward line second to none in the history of the game. In July that year they made a somewhat surprise move when they bought centre-forward Bobby Owen from Bury. I asked Booth the reasoning behind this, to which he replied, 'At the time we had good relationships with Bury – after all it was where we got Colin Bell from. Bobby had a tremendous track record and was knocking in goals left, right and centre. Malcolm – and in later years Brian Clough – said that the time to buy players is when you are winning things.

'Unfortunately for Bobby he found it more difficult in the First Division and played only a handful of games before moving to Carlisle, where he began scoring again. Things don't always work out in football.'

Scottish full-back Arthur Mann was also bought that year (for a then club record fee of £65,000), and suffered a similar Maine Road career to that of Bobby Owen.

The City sides of Booth's career were renowned for their simplicity and the speed at which they played their games. Joe Mercer once said that he wasn't bothered who came and watched them train, and to assist them in their efforts, City called on the services of a top British sprinter.

Booth recalls: 'Every Monday morning, providing we had no midweek game, the training sessions were given by Derek Ibbotson. They were so severe that none of the players would dare go out on a Sunday night. We really did train hard, although to be fair, we did have some superb athletes.

'Alan Oakes, Tony Book (really deceptive for his age), Mike Summerbee, Mike Doyle – we all had to work to maintain our fitness, day in, day out, week after week. All except one anyway – Colin Bell.

'When we used to go back for pre-season training, we used to dread it. Colin would have an extra three or four weeks off because he'd normally been away on tour with the England party. All the lads used to think we'd have these extra weeks up on Colin.' Apparently nothing could be further from the truth. Booth continues, 'Colin never sweated, never breathed hard. We'd all be coughing and spluttering and falling down. Colin was just a complete natural.'

Including Booth himself, few, if any, professional footballers would readily admit to liking training. 'It was a case of knowing the importance of it and therefore having to do it,' he says. 'In order to gain any benefit, the hard work has to be done pre-season. Then it was just a matter of maintaining it throughout the season. All the lads would go through it – and we'd have plenty of fun along the way. It might sound cruel but we used to laugh at players who, some days, would be struggling, knowing that it would be their turn to laugh the next day.'

Although not describing this training as enjoyable, Booth remembers the sessions being 'something different'. 'Local people would turn up regularly at Wythenshawe Park to watch us train. Derek Ibbotson said at the time that there were some players who could quite easily have become international runners instead of footballers. Colin Bell was certainly one of them, but fortunately for City he didn't.'

He also praises the abilities of two other team members – skipper Tony Book and Mike Summerbee: 'For his age, Tony Book was phenomenal. In those days we had a great run of results against United, and even now, honest Reds will admit to me that not even George Best – great player that he was – could get the better of Tony.'

Booth claims that a big help in games for Tony Book was the tireless work and effort of Mike Summerbee. 'Mike would drop back deep and collect the ball from Tony. It was Tony's job to win the ball and get it to Mike, to get the attacks going. It was a great escape route for the defence.'

The bigger the match (and harder the opposition), the more Summerbee would enjoy it. 'He was a hard lad, Mike. He used to love playing against Leeds United and the likes of Billy Bremner. Thankfully he was playing for us and not against us!' jokes Booth nowadays.

As a young impressionable fan myself during these glory years, I used to make my way to home games on the number 76 bus from Lord Lane in Failsworth. On one particular game (a night match, if memory serves me well), I was shocked when I saw Tommy Booth board my bus near the Grand Hotel in the centre of Manchester. Here was the first-team centre-half (and if newspaper reports were to be believed, a future England player), going to a match in which he was playing on the bus! This was something I just couldn't understand. I thought that top-flight footballers had Jaguars and the like.

Not so, as Booth remembers. 'I couldn't drive then,' he told me. 'When I'd established myself in the senior side, Joe Mercer said he'd sort out lessons and a car for me, which he eventually did.'

On a personal note, I asked Tommy if he had any regular pre-match routines or superstitions. 'No, not really,' he told me, 'although occasionally whilst sat on the bench in the dressing-room before the game I would do some "keep-ups".'

'Sat down?' I asked, slightly taken aback.

'Oh yes,' he replied. 'I would regularly do between 30 and 40, left-right, left-right – many times in just my stockinged feet. It relaxed me.' This particular Booth party piece can still be viewed today, particularly at charity functions when he obligingly takes money off the sceptics. All in a good cause, of course.

Science and nutrition play key roles in the performance of a 1990s professional footballer. These factors were less significant in the days (not so long ago) when Booth was playing. He remembers, 'Years ago you could have a steak before the game. Then they found out it contained too much high protein and wasn't digested in time. The trend then went on to chicken, cornflakes, peaches and nowadays, pasta.' All these choices made no difference to Tommy Booth. 'On the morning of a match, right through lunch-time, all I would have was two slices of toast. I could never eat a proper meal before a match. It wasn't a nervous thing; it was simply because I never fancied it.'

Ten minutes after the game, however, things were different. 'I could eat anything then,' he quipped. 'The other lads couldn't eat for a couple of hours.'

Booth's career (as both an amateur and a professional) at Maine Road lasted 16 years, and in that time he scored 36 goals in 476 (+4) first team appearances. None of those goals was more important than that one at Villa Park.

On 4 October 1981 he moved – along with Gary Buckley – to Preston North End where Tommy Docherty was manager. After a spell as first team coach he became a non-contracted manager of the Deepdale side four years later. Former Blue (although largely Red) Brian Kidd worked with Tommy as his assistant.

In 1987, after being unable to persuade the enormous Preston board of 24 directors to spend £20,000 in order to bring Denis Irwin (yes, the same one) from Leeds, Booth resigned, leaving Kidd to take over. Apart from his involvement in soccer schools, Tommy Booth's career with football had finished, 22 years after it had begun.

After leaving Preston Tommy set up a sports trophy business back in Manchester with his brother Paul. This lasted about three years until Paul left the area. Once this venture was over, Tommy admits that he was at a bit of a loose end, not really knowing what to do next. Then, one day, a chance conversation on the golf course (Booth plays off 11) offered him the opportunity to work for Granada TV. It's a job he still has today.

'I love it,' he told me. 'I'm out all day in the van, installing TV's, videos and satellite systems. It's interesting work and I'm hardly ever in the office.' Just think, if you live in or near Middleton, 'the best footballing centre-half since Stan Cullis' could be installing your new video.

Tommy's son Darren is currently working for the club as manager of the souvenir shops, both at the ground and in the city centre. On Valentine's Day in 1996, his fiancée proposed to him over the public address system at Maine Road during half-time in the Blues' FA Cup tie with Coventry City. Darren accepted the proposal.

This is an example of the kind of family atmosphere which has returned to the club since Francis Lee's takeover in February 1994. Tommy is very proud of this and says 'We still have some get-togethers – occasionally deep into the night. A bit like Matlock 1969!'

Saturday, 22 March 1969

FA Cup semi-final at Villa Park

Manchester City	1	(Booth)
Everton	0	

MANCHESTER CITY	v.	EVERTON
Harry Dowd	1	Gordon West
Tony Book	2	Tommy Wright
Glyn Pardoe	3	Sandy Brown
Mike Doyle	4	Howard Kendall*
Tommy Booth	5	Brian Labone
Alan Oakes	6	Colin Harvey
Mike Summerbee	7	Jimmy Husband
Colin Bell	8	Alan Ball
Francis Lee	9	Joe Royle
Neil Young	10	John Hurst
Dave Connor	11	Johnny Morrisey
Bobby Owen	SUB	Tommy Jackson*

Attendance: 63,025

6

PAUL POWER

City v. Ipswich Town
FA Cup semi-final at Villa Park, 11 April 1981

All 12 games recorded in this book were chosen by the players themselves. Purely by coincidence, Paul Power was the third player who chose a 1–0 FA Cup semi-final victory at Villa Park. All three players scored the decisive goals.

Paul's game took place on Saturday, April 11 1981, seven days after Bob Champion had ridden Aldaniti to victory in the Grand National. He has many memories of events leading up to that day: 'In October 1980 City were without a win in their first 12 games and Malcolm Allison lost his job. He'd come in and made some fairly radical changes, introducing a lot of younger players, like Ray Ranson, Tommy Caton, Nicky Reid and Steve MacKenzie.

'Once these younger players had been brought in, he showed the door to the more established international players like Dave Watson, Asa Hartford and Mike Channon. His emphasis was very much on youth. With hindsight this was probably asking too much of the youngsters – especially so many at one time – and consequently we struggled to get results. We lost at Leeds and Malcolm was asked to leave the day after.'

His replacement at Maine Road was the Norwich City manager John Bond, who in his playing days had played with Allison at West

Ham. 'Things just took off then for the rest of the season,' recalls Power today. 'It was just a matter of confidence really. John Bond went out and bought Tommy Hutchison, Gerry Gow and Bobby McDonald. The signing of McDonald in particular allowed me to play in a left-sided midfield position, which was really the one I preferred. Up until that point I'd been playing mainly at left-back.'

Despite these wholesale changes and the arrival of a new manager, Power remembers the atmosphere at Maine Road not being as gloomy as one might imagine: 'With the possible exception of a couple of players, the atmosphere was great. On the whole, people were disappointed that Malcolm had lost his job. They could see what he was trying to do and the way things were going.

'He'd introduced a lot of new ideas into the training schedule. We used to travel to the games on a Saturday morning, when we would do a spot of training, and then we'd all go to a hotel for a big breakfast. Malcolm changed the whole routine and for some of the old pros it was a little bit more difficult to cope with.

'He gave me my chance to captain the side and he stood by me pretty much all the time. When John Bond had watched a couple of games he took me to one side and told me that if I carried on with the same attitude there would be no problems in me keeping the job. I was quite pleased personally at the way things worked out.'

Because of the position City found themselves in, Bond's actions had to be quick and decisive. Power agrees: 'Yes, they did, but all he really did was to introduce those three players. As I've said, Bobby McDonald slotted in at number three, therefore releasing me to play further forward. Gerry Gow instilled the missing "steel" into the middle of the park, and Tommy Hutchison brought a bit of culture to the right-hand side. We hadn't really had a top quality right-sided player since Colin Bell retired.

'All the other players were kept on, and remember we also got through to the semi-final of the League Cup that year. We lost 2–1 to Liverpool over two legs and were very unlucky. Most of the team was made up of the players Malcolm had left behind; Dave Bennett and Tony Henry for instance. All of them made a contribution.'

The Blues lost their first two games under Bond, but then on 22 October, a 3–1 home win against Tottenham began a run of four consecutive wins. These included 15 goals and the 5–1 destruction of

Notts County in the League Cup. These results boosted everyone, especially the younger players. 'Once we'd started moving up the league a little, these younger players – who'd struggled at the beginning of the season – began to blossom. By the time the FA Cup semi-final came around, we were really on a high.'

In somewhat unusual circumstances, Malcolm Allison was back at Maine Road for the third round with his new side Crystal Palace. The Blues won 4–0 before inflicting a six goal whitewash on John Bond's former side Norwich City in the fourth round. Tommy Booth's goal was enough to win a potentially tricky away tie at Peterborough, and then two games were required to dispose of Everton in the quarter-final. With the exception of that Peterborough game, Paul Power had scored in every one of City's FA Cup games so far. 'Personally it had already been a great cup campaign,' recalls Power today. 'We had two very difficult games against Everton and we really didn't want to draw Ipswich in the semi-final. They were on such a good run at the time – they were going for the treble. They were in the FA Cup semi-final, involved in Europe and were going neck and neck with Aston Villa for the championship.

'Ipswich at that time had a very, very good side – managed, of course, by Bobby Robson – and they had a problem player for City: Eric Gates. We seemed to struggle against him every time.

'Their midfield was exceptional – a sort of diamond formation. It was made up of Arnold Muhren and Frans Thijssen who played wide, with John Wark and Eric Gates in the middle.'

On paper Ipswich were the more fancied side, but, as Power himself says, 'Confidence is a big thing in football – and we had plenty of that.' As expected, Ipswich began the game the stronger and more stylish side. Fortunately for City however, they struggled to do what they had been doing easily all season and that was score goals. Even the apparently irritating Eric Gates missed a great opportunity he would normally have expected to have put away. It is hardly surprising that some 15 years after the event, Paul finds it difficult to remember exact details of the game itself. 'It was a hot day and the pitch was very firm, and I remember all the City fans packed into the Holt End. The atmosphere was electric.'

Tommy Hutchison played for the Blues despite a pelvic injury, and City were put under considerable pressure early on. It was eased slightly when the Ipswich defender Kevin Beattie left the field injured after 25 minutes. 'This was a great bonus for us,' remembers Power. 'We'd been struggling at corners and set pieces because, with the exception of Tommy Caton, we had a relatively small defence. They had some good headers of the ball: players like Paul Mariner, John Wark and Russell Osman, as well as Beattie. The loss of Beattie gave us a big lift.' Before Beattie's injury he had almost given Ipswich the lead from one of those set pieces. He rose unchallenged inside the penalty area but so powerful was his downwards header that it bounced over the bar.

Power continues: 'There weren't many clear chances for either side throughout the match. I can't honestly remember Joe Corrigan and Paul Cooper having much to do. The game certainly wasn't like the replayed final against Spurs when chances were created at both ends almost from the kick-off.

'I suppose seven times out of ten that Ipswich side would have beaten us. Who knows, maybe we just caught them on a bad day, but none of us fancied the idea of a replay.'

When the referee blew his whistle at the end of 90 minutes, at least one person in the ground was prepared for that replay. That person was Eric Gates. 'At the end of the 90 minutes, Gates took his boots off, put them under his arm, and began to walk off,' recalls Power. 'I said to him that there was another half an hour to go yet. Gates said, "No, it's a replay, isn't it?" to which I replied, "No, there's extra-time." Gates then surprised me by saying "Oh no, you can have it!"'

This was another big boost to the captain's confidence. 'I thought well, let's hope they all feel the same. As far as we were concerned, we were all champing at the bit – waiting to get on with it.'

Once extra-time had arrived, Power still thought City were in with a chance. 'We had a young side – younger than theirs – and we had players who were good athletes. Nicky Reid and Tommy Caton would run all day, whilst Kevin Reeves was always comfortable holding the ball up, waiting for support. It was a well-balanced side. We had width on both the right and the left, and Gerry Gow's bite in the middle. He was a good buy for the club and his passion and enthusiasm rubbed off on the others.'

Eleven minutes into extra-time, City won a free-kick just outside the Ipswich penalty area. Paul Power takes up the story: 'What normally happened in these situations was Steve MacKenzie would knock a short sideways pass towards me. If it was on for a shot then I'd shoot, but if a player came off the wall to block me, I would roll it sideways again for Tommy Caton to strike with his left foot. This was a routine we worked on regularly in training.

'On this occasion Steve MacKenzie rolled it to me and no one came off the wall. They didn't work to close the ball down. I thought "in for a penny", and just whipped it in with my left foot. Paul Cooper was in goal and although he was a good shot-stopper, he was on the small side and just couldn't get his fingers to it. I remember the Holt End erupting in a sea of blue and white.'

Reporter Derek Wallis covered the semi-final for *The Daily Mirror*. His article was headed 'The Sky Blue Miracle' and it claimed to be 'Beyond Bond's belief'. It continued:

In the moment of triumph when Villa Park's precincts were still awash with sky blue, John Bond showed a touch of humility and humanity rare in managers in expressing his sorrow for Ipswich. 'It really is a shame,' he said for the umpteenth time. 'They're a much better team than they were today.' Perhaps he stated the obvious but he repeated it so often it was easy to form the impression that he couldn't really believe what had happened.

The history of football is littered with clubs which have recovered from adversity but I doubt if there has ever been a more dramatic example than Manchester City this season. 'It's a miracle,' said Peter Swales, admitting that had Bond failed, he would have had to consider resigning as chairman. He exaggerated, of course, in suggesting that some supernatural agency had intervened on City's behalf, but in the circumstances it was understandable and forgivable.

City have achieved the impossible dream almost as if the club had been transported to a fantasy island even more outrageous than the TV portrayal. I doubt, though, if many in the huge cliff of sky blue who greeted Paul Power's winning goal in extra-time, a shot struck wickedly from Steve MacKenzie's short free-kick, really believed during the opening half-hour that City had much of a chance. During a period which in the end was decisive, Ipswich showed in every respect except the most important one why they have been the team of the season with a one-touch economy and a persuasive style that threatened to sweep City aside arrogantly. The vital missing aspect was the inability to convert superiority into goals, with Eric Gates and Alan Brazil missing the sort of chances they would normally accept without thought.

City struggled in their wake, hopefully hitting long passes in a manner that at once both exaggerated and negated Bond's instructions to get the ball forward as quickly as possible. Russell Osman, Terry Butcher and Kevin Beattie simply stood there and picked them off almost contemptuously.

At that stage I wouldn't have given an old Maine Road programme for City's chances. They really needed one of Peter Swales's miracles. In the end, though, it was the more usual human error and endeavour. Ipswich, having already encountered unscheduled difficulty in scoring, developed incurable faults which spread to both the minds and the limbs, while at last City began to piece their game together.

Nicky Reid, who played possibly his most influential game, Tommy Caton and Bobby McDonald kept the Ipswich forwards in check. Skipper Power, whose floating style was in stark contrast to Gerry Gow's bristling aggression, enabled City to control the midfield where Tommy Hutchison's pelvic strain prevented him from playing with his usual perception.

If extra-time was a bonus to City it was a sentence of hard labour on Ipswich, who were clearly drained to the point of exhaustion. Even the token fightback after Power's goal 11 minutes into extra-time was born more of instinct than optimism.

Only eight players have played more times for City than Paul Power, and although he remembers the Ipswich game as his moment of Blue Heaven, he doesn't rate that goal as his best. 'It could have gone anywhere, basically,' he suggests. 'I struck it well enough but I honestly feel the goal I scored at Everton in the previous round was a better one.

'Dennis Tueart threaded me through and I'd gone past the defence. I had a lot of time to think about it. The goalkeeper was coming to close me down, but I was delighted with such a composed finish. It would have been more suited to Dennis actually who was better at that sort of thing.'

He continues, 'The situation with a semi-final is you either win everything or you lose everything. The old adage of "it's worse to lose in the semi than the final" is certainly true. I remember chairman Peter Swales saying at the reception shortly before the final, "It is better to have been there and lost, than never to have been there at all."

'Whilst this is obviously true, none of us wanted to lose at Wembley, and I just wonder even today, whether the disappointment of Tommy Hutchison's own goal on the Saturday was still with us on the Thursday. We were so near and yet so far.'

Ever since his early years Power had been a spectacle wearer, but for games would change into contact lenses. Without either form of assistance he does admit to being terribly short-sighted. 'I used to have several nicknames at City – all related to my short-sightedness. Alan Oakes, for instance, christened me "Grasshopper" from the Kung Fu TV series, whilst Mike Doyle would call me "Magoo".'

It was during the summer of 1976 that Paul Power began his one and only pre-match superstition. 'I went on my first trip abroad – to Japan and South Korea. Korea was a dreadful place and I decided I wasn't going to risk shaving. I didn't shave at all in Korea and scored three goals in three games. After that I never shaved at all on match days.'

On a personal note, 1981 was a good year for Paul Power. 'Early on in that year I won my only cap. I played for England B against Spain B in a game we lost 3–2 over there. My semi-final goal was in April, and then I led the side out twice at Wembley in May. Shortly afterwards I won City's Player of the Year award for the first time, and I got married in June. Yes, an awful lot happened to me that year.'

1981 was Power's eighth year associated with Manchester City Football Club. He was another talented young footballer spotted by the eagle eyes of City's former chief scout, the late Harry Godwin. 'Harry had seen me playing for a Sunday league team called West Park Albion. One day we were playing in the Manchester Cup competition against a side in Blackley, and Harry, living nearby, had just gone onto the playing fields. I was probably about 12 at the time.

'He later came to my house in Woodhouse Park and I answered the door. He asked if my dad was in and I told him no – he'd just popped down to his local, The Cock of the North, for a drink. Harry went down to the pub, met my dad and I was invited down for trials. City used to train at Cheadle then, and I would go down every Tuesday and Thursday night and train with a couple of old pros called Dick and Fred – Dick Neilson and Fred Kenny. They used to look after me.

'About that time I stopped growing, and although I used to do all the running and training, I never got a game at the end of it. I got disillusioned with everything and left.

'Later on I was playing for Manchester Boys Under 18s team against Ayrshire Boys at Brantingham Road and once again Harry was at the game. He had another word with my dad who was also there, saying "Ask him to come down again and we'll give him a game with the A and the B teams."' By this time Paul was about 17 years old and had applied to study law: 'I applied to two polytechnics – Kingston-upon-Thames and Leeds – and was accepted by both. The fact that City offered me games for the A team influenced my decision. Leeds being nearer meant I could travel home easily and play.'

Alongside his studying, Power progressed into City's reserve side where he played for two years whilst still in Leeds. 'If we ever had a midweek game,' he told me, 'for instance up at Newcastle, I would meet Dave Ewing (reserve team coach at the time) on the train in Leeds. Fortunately most reserve team games then were played on Saturday mornings so it meant I could travel home on Fridays. My mum and dad had a pub in Salford at the time, so I would earn a few bob helping out behind the bar. With City paying my travelling expenses, I suppose I was quite wealthy for a student.'

Power was also playing regular Wednesday afternoon football for the law department in the polytechnic's inter-departmental league. This was an ideal way of keeping fit; the design of his timetable was another. 'We had no lectures on Monday mornings, so this meant I wouldn't have to travel back to Leeds until lunch-time.

'Every Monday morning City held training sessions in Wythenshawe Park; these were just running days, so this was perfect for me. It provided an opportunity for me to meet and work with some of the first team players. All the teams would be involved in these sessions and it was great for me to be running against players I had idolised not too many years earlier. It really focused me – I thought: "This is the level I want to be at."'

He finally reached that level on 27 August 1975 when he made his debut for the first team. City lost 1–0 away to Aston Villa – a game played on the same Villa Park pitch that would see Power's greatest moment nearly six years later.

On 27 June 1986 – after 436 (+9) appearances and 35 goals – Paul Power, somewhat surprisingly perhaps, left Maine Road and moved to Everton. 'Yes, I suppose it was a bit of a shock,' he remembers, 'especially as I'd just signed a new one-year deal. But, looking back, it was probably good business for the club. I was 32 at the time and Andy Hinchcliffe was coming through the ranks. If I'd stayed for those 12 months I'd have been eligible for a free transfer. Billy McNeill looked at all the possibilities and decided to accept Everton's offer of £75,000.'

He found out about the move in somewhat peculiar circumstances: 'I was away on holiday in Devon at the time with my wife Julie who was pregnant. I've no idea how anybody knew where I was because I hadn't told anyone, but Jimmy Frizzell called me at the hotel. He told me Howard Kendall had been in touch with regard to a possible move.

'Billy McNeill was in Mexico at the time doing some TV work for the World Cup and Jimmy had phoned him to keep him in the picture. Billy gave permission for Howard Kendall to speak to me and so we had a meeting. There was nothing to lose as I still had the one-year deal with City.

'Everton had a really good side then so that didn't cause a problem, but there was still a complication about my testimonial at Maine Road. I'd been promised a testimonial game against United back in 1984, but the police refused to supervise it and a new date had still to be fixed. Howard Kendall promised me that if I signed he would bring an Everton side to Maine Road to play in my testimonial. And that's exactly what happened. I was actually an Everton player when I played my testimonial game at City; I played half the game for Everton, and half for City.'

Within 12 months of his move to Goodison Park, Paul Power was the proud owner of a championship medal. He recalls, 'When I signed I was told I could play anywhere on the left-hand side. When I looked more closely, however, I saw they had Pat Van Den Hauwe at full-back and Kevin Sheedy on the wing. For all intents and purposes it looked like I'd be a squad member.

'As things worked out, though, Howard obviously knew Pat had a problem with his ankle and so I started off at left-back. I played half the season there before Pat regained full fitness and then Kevin Sheedy got injured so I took his place.

'I played in 40 of the 42 league games that season – the only two I missed were the last two. I had a problem with my knee which needed an operation, so I decided I would give myself longer to recover in the summer by missing those last two games. The knee never really mended properly and I played just another 14 games the following season before moving on to the coaching staff.' He began his new career by looking after Everton's youngsters, a job he did with another former player, Mick Lyons. When Kendall moved to Spain in 1987, Colin Harvey took over the manager's reigns, and Power was promoted to first team coach.

By Power's own admission, the Everton sides of the late 1980s struggled to maintain the successes of Kendall's sides just a few years previously. This was hardly surprising, not to mention difficult for the current players, when you realise that in a six-year period, Everton had won four trophies and finished runners-up on three other occasions.

Kendall spent just over two years with Atletico Bilbao (and 11 months with City) before returning to Goodison Park for a second spell as manager in November 1990. His return brought about the usual shake-up of backroom staff. Colin Harvey was kept on as first team coach, but unfortunately Paul Power and several others lost their jobs.

Power would not be out of work for too long. 'From Goodison I got a job working with the "Football in the Community" Programme. I never really planned what I was going to do when I stopped playing. At one time I used to spend a couple of afternoons a week working in a law practice in Manchester with Mr Horwich. I thought I might go back to law when I'd finished with football.' (Avid readers of City's match-day magazine will have seen the name Michael Horwich before – he is the club's Honorary President.)

Power continued: 'Eventually the football commitments took up most of my time, making it impossible for me to follow a case through to its conclusion. I never thought about management at all. Coaching yes – I had all my qualifications – but management no.'

Nowadays Paul Power works for the PFA, having been seconded from the community programme in 1993. His present job title is

Coaching Administrator. 'Any coaching matters coming through the PFA are directed to me. These could be finding employment for former players who are qualified coaches, organising coaching education days or redesigning the coaching programme. I cover all aspects really. It is a very mixed bag.'

Power is responsible for these matters on a national basis and controls it all from a splendid suite of offices in the centre of Manchester. And he is still a City fan. 'I'd go to the games anyway, but I have this arrangement with BBC local radio, GMR. I watch all the home games and some of the aways, and there's a phone-in afterwards. My job with the PFA gives me plenty of inside knowledge and because I'm expected to comment, I have to watch the games perhaps a bit more closely than the normal spectator does. I also enjoy speaking to the fans a great deal and listening to their opinions.'

Paul Power was undoubtedly a great servant for Manchester City Football Club. Indeed, he is still more than useful when turning out for City's Old Boys in charity games. 'I'm just a summer footballer nowadays,' he told me.

Does he have any other memories of that marvellous game back in 1981 – the 'Botham's Ashes' year of 1981? 'We came straight back after the game and got off the coach at the Post House in Northenden. The manager looked after us really well with plenty of champagne flowing.

'Around nine o'clock we all went our separate ways – I went to meet my fiancée Julie – so it wasn't a real late-nighter. Mind you, we did drink an awful lot in a period of about three hours. It was a great day.'

On a final, perhaps philosophical note, Paul Power told me, 'The important thing about that goal is that all the City supporters of the era remember it. Whenever people see me, even today, they always remember that one goal. I sometimes think if I hadn't scored that goal they might not have remembered me for much.'

I doubt it, Paul, I doubt it.

Saturday, 11 April 1981

FA Cup semi-final at Villa Park

Manchester City	1	(Power)
Ipswich Town	0	
after extra-time		

MANCHESTER CITY	v.	IPSWICH TOWN
Joe Corrigan	1	Paul Cooper
Ray Ranson	2	Mick Mills
Bobby McDonald	3	Terry Butcher
Nicky Reid	4	Frans Thijssen
Paul Power	5	Russell Osman
Tommy Caton	6	Kevin Beattie*
David Bennett	7	John Wark
Gerry Gow	8	Arnold Muhren
Steve MacKenzie	9	Paul Mariner
Tommy Hutchison	10	Alan Brazil
Kevin Reeves	11	Eric Gates
Tommy Booth	SUB	Steve McCall*

Attendance: 46,537

7

MIKE SUMMERBEE

City v. Preston North End
Football League Division Two at Deepdale, 23 October 1965

The First Division Championship, FA Cup victory, Football League Cup triumph, glorious European Cup Winners' Cup Wednesday nights – with the exception of the Cup Winners' Cup final in Vienna which he missed through injury, in 441 (+2) games spread over ten years in City's colours, Mike Summerbee has seen and done it all. Which game would he choose then as his idea of Blue Heaven?

'I remember a marvellous match against Atletico Bilbao – but it's not that one.'

Which one, then?

'It was such a long time ago but I still have fond memories of it.'

Which game is it?

'City versus Preston North End at Deepdale in Division Two back in October 1965.'

City versus Preston – Division Two!

'For lots of reasons. I was a Prestonian, going back to where my dad played and was respected, Tom Finney was in the stand watching and it was the first time I'd been back to Preston as a player.'

The game took place on Saturday 23 October (the height of the Moors Murders enquiries) in front of a crowd of 25,117. It was City's 13th game of the season – a season which so far had seen them lose just once and one which would finish with the Second Division championship.

Summerbee had arrived at Maine Road on 20 August that year from Swindon Town for the unbelievable bargain fee of £35,000. His debut came the following day in the opening game of the new season. It was a 1–1 draw at Middlesbrough, and Summerbee provided the cross for Jimmy Murray's goal. That game was also the first time substitutes could be used, the honour for City falling to Glyn Pardoe.

Describing the game at Deepdale, Summerbee remembers, 'It was just one of those games when everything went right for me. I remember their full-back, a Scot named John Donnelly. He never touched the ball all day!' Preston had not lost at home since November the previous year. The team that had beaten them 5–2 that day was George Poyser's Manchester City, thanks to two goals from Neil Young and a Derek Kevan hat-trick. Deepdale proved to be a happy hunting ground for Neil Young because he found the net twice more in 1965. The Blues went ahead after 20 minutes through Scottish inside-forward Ralph Brand. (Incidentally, Ralph Brand has the honour of being Joe Mercer's first signing for City, and not Mike Summerbee as is often quoted. Brand had signed from Glasgow Rangers nine days before Summerbee put pen to paper.)

Good work by Young and the ever-dependable Glyn Pardoe enabled Brand to slip the ball past the advancing Alan Kelly in the Preston goal. All three players involved in the goal would be guilty later on of failing to extend City's lead from clear-cut opportunities. It was looking like one of those days – easier to score than miss – and despite City's overwhelming authority they had to content themselves with a one-goal lead at the break. 'It really was a great game,' Summerbee recalls over a cup of coffee in the Oasis Suite. 'There are lots of other games you can pick out, but for sheer pleasure, to go back to where my father had played, to where I was born, to play on the same wings as the great Tom Finney and give a good performance – it was a marvellous day.

'Of course I didn't play the same stylish way as Tom played but I have to say that on that day, my way was devastating. It was one of those days when the full-back just couldn't compete with me at all. That's no disrespect to him; everything went right for me and nothing went right for him. Whatever I did, Donnelly had no answer.

'There was another game I played in against Leicester City in similar circumstances to the Preston game. On that particular day their full-back was substituted, and as he was leaving the pitch Francis Lee said to him, "You can open your eyes now, the nightmare's over!" The same thing could have been said to the poor guy at Preston. I had everything to play for. Although I didn't have to prove anything, it was nice to go back to a place and put the Summerbee name back on the map.'

The second half continued along the same lines as the first, with City spending long periods laying siege to the Preston goal but still unable to increase their lead. This inability led to frustration on the terraces and police moved in to evict several angry City fans from the ground. Meanwhile other, more peaceful and contented Blues followers, began to sing 'We're going up' – arrogant and confident chanting when you think there was still seven months and 29 league games to go until the end of the season!

City continued to miss chances – many created by Summerbee – until the 77th minute when Neil Young finally made it 2–0. (Shortly before Young's goal City had had three penalty appeals in three minutes turned down.) With just two minutes to go Young struck his second and City's third and the game was over. The scoreline at last portrayed a more honest picture of the afternoon, although many people thought City were so superior that a winning margin of ten would have been a clearer indication. Newspaper reports claimed that 'City were inspired by Summerbee', who in turn was described as 'superb'.

City's historian John Maddocks also has memories of that trip to Deepdale. 'I was a teacher at the time in Brinnington and I took a car full of lads up to Preston. On the way back in the car I kept hearing a loud cracking noise. It took me ages to find out what it was. After a while I turned round and was horrified to see one of the lads firing an airgun out of the window!'

Born in Preston on 15 December 1942, Summerbee had moved to Cheltenham as a youngster. 'My father was manager of Cheltenham Town. One of his players at the time was a centre-forward called Roy Shirer. Shirer moved to Huddersfield Town and later Sheffield Wednesday, where he scored something like 100 times in 150 games. Cheltenham always seemed to have a useful side.

'My dad, of course, had also played. He was a full-back and played at Preston having joined them from Aldershot in 1935. After the war he moved to Chester for a season and finished his career at Barrow after 120-odd matches. I had an uncle who played for Aldershot as well.

'When Nick [Mike's son] made his debut for Swindon in 1989, he was the third generation Summerbee to play league football. There have never been three before; there have been fathers and sons – but never grandfather, father and son. I can't think of another family that's achieved that – even in Europe, let alone in Britain.'

Back to Deepdale in October 1965. 'That's what football is all about. It's easy for players to pick the games that people think about. The thing is, we've each chosen games that were important to us, whether it be a lift off in our careers, a coming of confidence, a disappointment or whatever. With such a mixture it all makes for interesting reading for the fans. Anyone can pick out the really big, successful games all the time, but by the time you've read three or four it becomes a bit monotonous. People think, "I've had enough of this." What you're looking at here is a real insight into what a player thinks and feels.

'When I came to Manchester City the club was at a very low ebb. I'd played here the season before for Swindon in front of just 8,000, but that City side of 1965–66 was as good a Second Division side as you could possibly come across. You had players that had been together for quite a long time such as Mike Doyle, Alan Oakes, Roy Cheetham and Cliff Sear. They all became lifted. Instead of being down all the time, suddenly they started to believe in themselves. They worked together very, very well in different ways and Joe and Malcolm provided the confidence that made them into a successful unit.

'This particular game at Preston I think was the coming of age of that team. It certainly was my coming of age. I'd come to a big club and I have to say that at first I did feel a bit insecure. As well as the players mentioned, Derek Kevan was here, along with Jimmy Murray, Bobby Kennedy and Ralph Brand. All these were great players whom I'd seen play, and they had big reputations. To be actually playing with them was great, but I had to prove myself to them as well as to the fans. This game proved for me that I could compete at the highest level and then go on from there.

'Not only was the game important for me because I had an exceptional game, but I think the team realised then what potential we had and what could be achieved. The other important thing for me was the Preston connection, along with the fact that I'd played so well when the great Tom Finney was watching. Ever since I was an 18 month-old baby I'd been taken to Tom's house so I'd already known him for a long time.

'On a recent holiday to Portugal I went into a restaurant for Sunday lunch and, much to my surprise, Tom was in there. We had a good, long chat, and I happened to mention to him that I didn't have a photograph of my father in Preston's colours. "No problem – leave it to me," said Tom. Two weeks after I'd come home, a photo of my father with the famous "P.P." badge on his chest dropped through my letter box. That is the mark of Tom Finney. Not only was he a great footballer, but to this day, he can always find time for other people.'

Throughout Summerbee's playing career which lasted almost 20 years, he always carried the reputation of being a hard man as well as a character. 'I did something I always liked doing,' he recalls. 'It was never difficult for me to play football – remember that I was brought up in a football family. It was an ambition of mine to play at the highest level. At Swindon the manager Bert Head expected you to survive and get stuck in. In my early days – I'd have been about 16 – I pulled out of a few tackles and then one day in front of all the senior players he said to me, "If I see you do that again you'll never play another game for me." So the next time we played I went into a tackle, closed my eyes, and came out without being injured. I suppose that's really how I came to be an aggressive kind of player. I never broke anybody else's leg, but I did break mine – twice!

'I just competed. People always think it's defenders who are the hard men of football, but that's not the case. The hard men are the forwards. Wingers in particular have this reputation of being cowards but I wasn't. It was never my intention to injure anybody. It was just the way I played the game.

'As far as being a character is concerned, yes, I did get some ribbing from the oppositions' supporters. But the way I look at it is this: they only ribbed the people who could play. I had a banter with the fans because that's the way I am, that's the way I enjoy things. My concentration never wandered because of it.

'I felt that with me playing on the wing I could have a chat with the crowd or the linesman or whoever. Nowadays of course you can't do that. You'd be booked, charged with bringing the game into disrepute or accused of inciting a riot. Over the years football supporters have changed. During my time there was no hint of any violence and you could do these things for a bit of fun. You could put your arm around a linesman, take his flag off him and have a laugh and that was it. You daren't do it today, though.

'I'm all for a bit of fun, but some of the things they get up to after a goal these days are just plain silly and embarrassing. In my day, when you congratulated a player you just put your arm around him or patted him on the back. You never did any of the crazy, jumping around stuff. It's only to bring attention to themselves. If you're not on television very much, you do something like that and then there you are, you get yourself on television. I think the same could be said about referees as well. I'm sure they book players sometimes just so their families can see them on television. If a referee controls a game properly, nobody ever sees him.

'Having said that, though, I do have some sympathy for referees. They are under so much pressure, what with television replays and the new laws, that the slightest thing a player does, the referee must be seen to be charging him with something. Take that ridiculous Paul Gascoigne incident with the yellow card, for instance.' (He is referring to the occasion when 'Gazza' took the referee's yellow card, pretended to book him and was promptly booked himself by the unimpressed referee.) Mike continued: 'That's the reason why there are no real characters in the game anymore. By characters I mean people who just do things off the cuff – on the spur of the moment with no planning.'

A man always willing to talk honestly about football, Mike was asked if his father's footballing prowess was in any way forced on to him. He replied, 'My father died when he was 39; I was 11 at the time and my brother was 12. We got our new football boots for Christmas because we wanted them. We were no different from any other children apart from being able to take part in "England versus Scotland" games.

'At the time there were about eight Scottish internationals – the likes of George Mutch, Bill Shankly, Andy Beattie and Bobby Beattie – playing for Preston and I remember our "internationals" played on the local recreation ground.' It was perhaps fitting then that the first of Summerbee's eight 'proper' England caps was won against Scotland at Hampden Park in February 1968.

'There was never any pressure on me then just as there's no pressure on Nick now. You're either good enough at the game or you're not. It has perhaps been more difficult for Nick because he's done the same trip as me, playing for Swindon and then coming here. Now, though, he is definitely his own person.

'He's had that "He's only here because of his dad" bit, but it's not true. He's here because he's an exceptional player. Before people here think you can play, you've got to put the ball in the net, but that's not his way. He's a provider and he does a good job. You take him out of the side and you'll notice a difference. I think he's the best crosser of the ball at the club.

'When I played, my crosses would always seem to find either Wyn Davies or Francis Lee. Sometimes though nobody gets on the end of Nick's crosses and in that situation it looks like a misplaced pass. That's when he gets criticised.

'There are lots of people writing today in newspapers who've no idea what the game is all about. Players who are having a rough time – as most invariably do during their careers – need a bit of encouragement and not the kind of comments that are written in the papers. It seems that all they want to write about are the bad things – the controversial things. I suppose that in the 1990s that sort of story sells papers. It has to be said, though, that not all clubs are treated in the same way by certain members of the press. Anyway that's another story . . .'

See, I told you he talked honestly about football!

In the late 1960s City were undoubtedly the best team in the country, and winning silverware became a regular and even expected event. Less than three years after Summerbee's most memorable game, City were First Division champions. That same year – 1968 – Manchester United won the European Cup when they beat Portuguese champions Benfica 4–1 at Wembley. It has to be said that United too had a good side. Not as good as ours, but nevertheless quite useful.

These two achievements confirmed Manchester as the footballing capital of the country. With this success came music, fashion and nightclubs and for a while 'swinging London' was put on hold. This was the Manchester of crushed velvet jackets, boutiques and George

Best. To this day George Best and Mike Summerbee are good friends, the friendship having been formed during their playing days. In 1967 it produced a business partnership – the Edwardia boutique in the centre of Manchester. 'I got into the shirt business in 1969,' recalls Summerbee today. 'I met a cutter who worked in Manchester for a big London shirt manufacturer. He made some shirts for me and I thought it might be a business I could get into. I took on a partner who looked after the business whilst I was playing, but unfortunately that didn't work out so I just took it on from there.

'The cutter retired and I had a young boy who worked for me for a long time. He then set his own company up – James Ashcroft, Shirtmaker – and they're now probably the best shirtmakers in Manchester. All I do is sell the shirts he makes for me and I pay him per shirt. It's nothing like the size of business Francis Lee built up when he was playing. Mine's only a small business, dealing entirely with individuals, not with shops. They are all bespoke shirts.'

There's an old footballing joke that even today rears its head on occasions.

Question: Who is the last City player to play in Europe ?

Answer: Mike Summerbee in *Escape to Victory*.

The answer, of course refers to a 1981 movie shot in Hungary, concerning an Allied escape attempt from a German prisoner-of-war camp. Football is used as a diversion tactic in the movie which starred Michael Caine and Sylvester Stallone. Someone in Hollywood realised that for authenticity some actors should actually be able to play. These 'actors' included Bobby Moore, Pele, Osvaldo Ardiles and City stars Kazi Deyna and Mike Summerbee. I asked Mike how all this came about.

'Bobby Moore got me into it,' he replied. 'I'd known Bobby for years – our families are very close – and one day he just asked me if I fancied doing this film he was involved with. Naturally I said yes and that was that. Because of that film I now make shirts for Michael Caine, Sylvester Stallone and Max von Sydow. There's a company in London run by a lady called Andrea Gaylor which provides costumes for films. Whenever there's something special to be made I make it for her. I recently made some shirts for John Hurt.

'I have my shirt business to run which means I can't spend every day with Geoff Durbin, the commercial manager, but he knows that.

We work well together and I do what I can. I can talk to people, sell them something and they all seem to like to meet the former players. As well as that it's good public relations for the club.'

Mike Summerbee has come a long way since working as a deck-chair attendant on the Torquay sea-front in the summer of 1965. His footballing talents were about to outgrow the rural setting of Swindon Town. 'At that time there was a lot of talk in newspapers linking me to both Leicester City and Tottenham. Managers of both clubs – Matt Gillies and Bill Nicholson – both knew my father, as did Joe Mercer. In fact Joe had actually tried to sign me when he was in charge at Aston Villa.

'Tottenham offered £12,000 for me but Swindon turned it down. When City bid I was delighted. Despite the fact that the club had been having a lean time I wasn't bothered. Joe Mercer was the difference for me.'

Summerbee's first season for City – in which he played all 42 league games – finished with City winning the Second Division championship, five points clear of their nearest rivals Southampton. 'Hey, that wasn't all down to me!' says Summerbee. 'There were some good players there and Joe Mercer and Malcolm Allison made them believe in themselves. It wasn't just Lee, Bell and Summerbee that made it tick.

'Every team must function as a team. There will always be individuals who will stand out, getting a bit of glory, because they've scored a goal, made a goal or won a game. But collectively, that Second Division side was one hell of a team.

'We had Johnny Crossan for instance – probably one of the greatest players this club has ever had. He might have been coming to the end of his career but he was well-travelled, had lots of experience and had played in Europe for Standard Liege as well as for Northern Ireland.

'Others like Alan Oakes, Neil Young and Glyn Pardoe had been here through the lean times and people thought they couldn't play. Suddenly with a change of management, personalities and training, they developed and became really good players.

'I think it was a great shame that David Wagstaffe left Maine Road. For me he was an exceptional player and I often wonder what it would have been like here had he stayed and worked with Joe and Malcolm.'

'Buzzer' was privileged to be part of the much-chronicled great sides produced by Joe Mercer and Malcolm Allison in the late '60s and early '70s. A combination of skill, fitness and, perhaps most important of all, team spirit, made these now legendary sides. 'It wasn't just the home games – everywhere we went we had a good "craic". We had a tremendous camaraderie. When we went to other grounds I would always have "We'll walk a million miles to the end of your nose" sung at me. People talk about racism today. I used to be told to "Get back to Israel", and I'm not even Jewish!

'But I used to accept all that – it was just banter, a bit of fun. They didn't mean it. I would get all sorts of things thrown at me but I realised I was in a position to be shot down and I just used to get on with it. I used to get spat at, and many times I've been called an ugly bastard. I got terrible stick at Anfield and Old Trafford, but I bet they both would have loved me to be playing for them! It's as simple as that.'

In February 1968 Summerbee, in an age when wingers were not in favour, made the step up to international football when he played centre-forward in that game at Hampden Park. Between that date and June 1973 he played eight times for his country, scoring just once – a looping header against Switzerland at Wembley.

On 13 July 1975 he left Maine Road and moved to Burnley for a fee of £25,000. 'City had had the best ten years of my career and they only lost £10,000 on the fee they paid for me. I think they got a good deal.

'The great City side was breaking up – Francis Lee had gone to Derby County for instance – and I realised I was coming to the end of my career. I couldn't give them my best any more. I really struggled most of the time.

'Earlier in the season Don Revie and Leeds were interested but Ron Saunders messed the deal up. Everything was ready and I was all set to go. Anyway in the summer I joined Burnley and in a way I'm glad the Leeds deal fell through. I spent 18 months at Turf Moor under Jimmy Adamson and had a brilliant time. I then went to Blackpool. That was a farce really – non-existent! Stockport was different, though – I enjoyed it there. I played 90-odd games for County – some as player-manager – before finally calling it a day.' Did he fancy the idea of becoming a full-time manager, either at Edgeley Park or somewhere else? 'No, thank you! The worst thing about being a manager is going into a board of directors who've never played the game and hearing them tell you how to do it.

'The thing about Alan Ball is he's got a chairman who has actually played, and at the highest level. When someone miscontrols a ball or things aren't going too well, the chairman knows exactly what the situation is. He won't just go straight in and criticise because he knows that sometimes football is not such a simple game.'

Simple, difficult and sometimes impossible. Whatever words are used to describe the game of football, things always seemed to be brighter and more enjoyable whenever Mike Summerbee was on the pitch. The ruffle of the hair, the tugging of his shirt cuffs before taking a corner-kick . . . whatever fans will remember about Mike Summerbee, to a man (or woman), they will all say he is entitled to be known as a great player.

Football League Division Two at Deepdale

Preston North End	0	
Manchester City	3	(Brand, Young 2)

PRESTON NORTH END	v.	MANCHESTER CITY
Alan Kelly	1	Harry Dowd
George Ross	2	Bobby Kennedy
John Donnelly	3	Cliff Sear*
Nobby Lawton	4	Roy Cheetham
Bill Cranston	5	George Heslop
Howard Kendall	6	Alan Oakes
Dave Wilson	7	Mike Summerbee
Brian Godfrey	8	Johnny Crossan
Alex Dawson	9	Glyn Pardoe
Alan Spavin	10	Ralph Brand
Willy Watt	11	Neil Young
Ernie Hannigan	SUB	Dave Bacuzzi*

Attendance: 25,117

8

COLIN BELL

City v. Newcastle United
Football League Division One at Maine Road, 26 December 1977

'My father was a good footballer. Nottingham Forest were interested in him until they found out he was 29 and then they gave him the cold shoulder. My mother played for a womens' team in the north-east, my sister played for a team and so did all my uncles.' It is hardly surprising with a background like this, that any baby born into the family would grow up liking football. Little did anyone know that the baby boy born on 26 February 1946, in the Durham mining village of Hesleden near Hartlepool, would become one of the finest players Britain has ever produced.

Colin Bell was that baby and he continues the story: 'My mother died when I was born and, because my dad was a miner working shifts, my sister had to look after me.' She would take the two-year-old Bell to school with her. 'I used to play in the school yard whilst my sister had lessons. She says that half the time the pupils would be looking out of the window watching me with the ball.'

Those very early practice sessions proved beneficial for Bell as, in later years, he was to turn out for both the Horden Colliery Welfare junior team and for East Durham Boys. Bell remembers his days with Horden: 'We had a cracking side. The two men who ran it were always scouting the area looking for the best players and signing them for us. We regularly beat teams 18–0 and 21–1.' It was during this time his talents were beginning to be noticed by the top league clubs. 'I had a trial with Newcastle – I played in their 'N' side – I must have been about 15 or 16. They weren't interested so I then had a trial with Arsenal, but the choice eventually came down to either Huddersfield or Bury.

'Along with my dad, I spent time at both clubs. I said that I wouldn't make my mind up whilst I was away, I'd go home and think about it. I played two reserve games for Bury – against Everton and Wolves – and these were my trial games. I remember two directors coming back to the hotel to get me to sign. They must have been there until about two o'clock in the morning with my dad, trying to get me to put pen to paper. I was determined not to commit myself, and anyway, I'd already promised Huddersfield I'd call them. They both offered me the same wages – a fortune at £12 a week!'

At this stage Newcastle showed renewed interest but were told, 'Oh no, you've had your chance.' Bell continues, 'Even so, I was 90 per cent certain I'd sign for Bury there and then. I was just a humble lad and the whole set-up at Bury was much more friendly and homely. That's really what decided it for me.'

What if Huddersfield had been more homely?

Would Colin Bell ever have played for City?

The prospects aren't even worth considering!

On 8 February 1964 Colin Bell made his debut in league football – for Bury against Manchester City at Maine Road. That game is also memorable for two other reasons: Colin Bell scored for Bury, and Harry Dowd, City's injured goalkeeper (playing up front with his arm in a sling), scored the Blues' equaliser.

Bell scored 25 times in 82 league games for Bury before signing for City on 16 March 1966. As with Bury and Huddersfield previously, again Colin had a decision to make. 'Two clubs wanted me – Blackpool and City. Blackpool were in the First Division, but at the wrong end and looked like they could be relegated.' (They actually finished the season in 13th place, but only four points clear of relegation.) City on the other hand were top of the second and looked odds-on for promotion. I wanted to play First Division football so I looked at both clubs – there was no choice really.'

There is a story about Malcolm Allison's determination to bring Colin Bell to Maine Road. 'Malcolm really wanted me. He came to watch me a couple of times at Bury and began to give out duff stories: "He can't pass, he can't head, he can't do this, and so on." As usual Malcolm took centre-stage and everyone around – knowing what a good judge he was – began to listen and believe him. Days later he signed me.'

The fee was £45,000, nowadays approximately two months' wages for a top Premier League player. 'That was a fortune to me back then,' recalls Bell as we sit talking in the Oasis Suite at the Platt Lane Complex. 'Remember I was 19, and I must admit that the fee did weigh heavily around my neck for a while.'

His City debut came in a 2–1 win at Derby County three days after his arrival – and again he scored. On 4 May he scored the goal that clinched the Second Division championship: 'Rotherham away. We won 1–0.' At this point I showed Bell a photograph of that vital goal: 'Neil Young's cross and I headed it in. I remember hurting my ankle and it swelled up. We didn't want to risk taking my boot off in case I couldn't get it back on again, so we just taped it up, right around my boot and ankle. Malcolm had been carrying the champagne around for ages ready for the promotion celebration. The changing-rooms at Rotherham were very small – just a wooden hut – but we still managed to drink it. I'd never seen champagne before; I didn't know what it was!'

He continues, 'My memory isn't as good as some of the others'. Francis and Mike, for instance, can remember precise details from games. In all honesty, when you've played as many games as I have there aren't very many which spring to mind. Most of them are much of a muchness. There are, however, certain ones that stick in my mind for particular points.

'During those great five or six years I could pick a few out – like the time we won the championship at Newcastle. But perhaps my biggest memory in all the time I played was a game when we didn't win anything. It was just a league game – also against Newcastle – when I came back from my knee injury. I'm not the kind of person who gets emotional even after scoring a goal – it's all part and parcel of the game – but I remember getting a big lump in my throat as I came down the tunnel that day. The kids were all leaning over the wall at Maine Road as the teams were coming out for the second half, and then I heard all the whispers going round. I got a standing ovation from both sets of supporters – all 45,000 of them.'

The game in question took place on Boxing Day 1977. Colin Bell was named as substitute. His wife Marie was reported to have said at the time, 'We were both terribly nervous. Colin couldn't even eat his Christmas dinner!' Their nervousness was understandable. It had been more than two years since Bell had figured in City's first team plans.

On 12 November 1975 the Blues beat Manchester United 4–0 in a fourth round League Cup tie at Maine Road. Poised for a shot on goal, Bell was challenged by United's Martin Buchan. The ensuing collision damaged knee ligaments, cartilage and blood vessels. Bell was immediately stretchered off and his injury overshadowed an otherwise memorable night.

During his two-year absence Bell spent literally hundreds of hours in the gym, running, stretching, working with weights – all in a valiant attempt to regain full fitness. 'Everybody at the club was marvellous,' recalls Colin. 'The manager Tony Book never lost faith in me and I had tremendous help from physios Freddie Griffiths and Roy Bailey.' Even chairman Peter Swales said, 'Colin Bell is the finest tuned athlete ever to have played for Manchester City and we want him back in the first team.' Bell also recalls losing all sense of time. 'When I was playing, I could always tell what day of the week it was by a Saturday. Without having that special day – the Saturday – I had no idea what day it was.' On his return Marie said, 'A big cloud has been lifted from him. He is like a different person – so much happier.'

The week before the Newcastle game, City had been beaten 2–0 at Leeds, where their bookings reached 25 for the season. By half-time City had been unable to break down the Geordies' defence and the game was goalless. An injury to Paul Power forced Tony Book to bring on his substitute. Bell remembers, 'I don't know how it came about – I was just told I was going out for the second half. At the time the game was a bit flat with nothing very much happening. When I came on I can't honestly remember touching the ball and we won 4–0. The atmosphere had seemed to go up a few notches since I came on, but I didn't do a thing. We played ten against eleven. It was the atmosphere – not me – that picked the players up. The game just passed me by.'

Whatever the reason, the Blues' second-half performance was too much for Newcastle. Dennis Tueart scored his third hat-trick of the season ('I knew he'd scored two – I didn't realise it was three!'), and

Brian Kidd netted the other. So good was Tueart's finishing that Tony Book described him as 'the best finisher in the business'. These goals took Tueart's tally to 14 for the season – five behind the league's leading scorer, Everton's Bob Latchford.

'We had a great spell of winning things at the end of the '60s,' remembers Bell, 'almost expecting to really. Championships, cups, European success, but that one game is perhaps my greatest memory. Probably because the standing ovation, the applause, the cheering – all that was for me personally. All the other ovations had been for the teams. Mind you, the fans have always been great with me at Maine Road, ever since day one.'

Three days after Bell's comeback game, Alec Johnson wrote the following piece in *The Daily Mirror*. Under the heading 'Happy Bell still below HIS target' the article went as follows:

> Everyone at Manchester City is jubilant over the return to match fitness of their former England hero Colin Bell. Everyone except Bell . . . the man who has fought for two years to get over a serious leg injury. The 31-year-old Bell told me yesterday, 'It is a great feeling to be back in action with the first team. But I won't be satisfied until I'm playing and fulfilling my old role with the side.'
>
> To practically everyone except Bell himself, his return to the first team over the Christmas period has been almost unbelievable. Although no one, understandably, would ever admit it, few people in football believed even the courageous Bell could overcome such a serious injury. Didn't even Bell slump to some lowest moment of despair when his lionheart outlook began to see dark defeat ahead? 'No, I never lost hope,' said Bell yesterday. 'It was a matter of patience and the whole thing was building up strength in the leg. I've had terrific help from the staff at Maine Road, especially from physiotherapist Freddie Griffiths and Roy Bailey his assistant. Along with manager Tony Book they have never lost faith in me and that has meant a lot.'
>
> Then Bell – renowned as an unemotional poker-faced character both on and off the field – recalled the moment when he stepped on as substitute for the second half against Newcastle United on Boxing Day. The 45,000 crowd gave him a fantastic ovation.

I'm not an emotional person,' he said. 'But that moved me more than anything that has happened in my life. It was staggering. I had never even thought that the fans felt like that about me. Long after the game I could still hear them cheering . . . '

Manager Tony Book is full of enthusiasm. 'Colin has worked and sweated to get back and no praise is too high. Other players would have quit long ago, I'm certain of that.'

Bell expects no favours, nor seeks them. 'It is up to the manager to consider if I'm worth a place in the team,' he emphasises. 'At the moment several men are out with injuries and obviously I've come in to replace them. What I want to do is get back to my old self – and fit back in the midfield role that I've always played in in the past. I want to prove I can be exactly the same player that I was.' And although Bell didn't say it, that sort of player is an automatic choice in any team . . .

'I wasn't worried about taking another knock on the knee,' Bell told me, 'but it was never ready. I played I don't know how many games after the injury, but the knee then is the same as it is now. It wouldn't bend so I couldn't travel at speed.

'I remember Tony Book played me in the reserves at Blackpool and I was getting to certain balls five yards after the Blackpool player had gone. I had to readjust mentally, I had to cut them off at the pass. Instead of going for the ball as I would have done had I been fit – or had my knee been right – I had to reassess the situation, and go somewhere else. I told Tony that if I wasn't fit and able to pull my weight, I didn't want to play in any side.'

Book played him again 24 hours after his comeback, away at Middlesbrough. City won 2–0 and Bell laid on the second goal for Gary Owen. Newspaper headlines read 'Bell rings out title warning'. The City boss was mightily pleased. 'Four points out of four and Colin Bell back,' reported *The Daily Mirror*. Book continued, 'Colin's return strengthens my hand tremendously and his very presence is a morale booster.'

The Blues' title hopes were blunted when their unbeaten run of nine games (eight wins and a draw) was halted at Arsenal. Bell recalls, 'I got another knock on the knee from a tackle on the half-way line. I think it was a clot of congealed blood from the original injury, and it just popped out of the side of the knee.

'That put me back again, but I was just grateful I could still walk. When I first had the injury I couldn't put any weight on it for about six or eight months. Then I went back to the ground to start work with Freddie Griffiths and Roy Bailey.

'When I put any weight on it – even an ounce – I had pins and needles the full length of my leg. I could not put my foot on the ground at all and I thought at one stage I would never walk again. But eventually I got past that stage and then every day was a big plus.'

The main part of his recovery time was spent at home with his young daughter Dawn and his wife Marie. He remembers, 'For about the first year or so all I did was sit in a chair with my leg strapped up, resting it on a stool. I'm not the sort of person who relies on others – I like to do things for myself – but I couldn't do anything. Even with little things like going into the kitchen for a meal, Marie would have to help me.'

Bell played just ten league games of the 1978–79 season, at the end of which Tony Book lost his job to the returning Malcolm Allison. He had a long, honest discussion about his fitness with Allison before finally announcing his retirement on 21 August 1979. His Maine Road career consisted of 489 (+3) league and cup appearances with 152 goals. Only five players have played more times for City, and only two players have scored more goals. He scored nine times in 48 games for England, making him City's most-capped international of all time.

Colin Bell suggests that, but for the injury, he could have played for another three or four years. 'Stamina was never the problem, it was just the mobility of the knee.' Other people think it could have been longer. Regardless of opinions, the injury to Colin Bell effectively robbed Manchester City and England of the talents of one of the country's most gifted footballers.

All through his playing career Colin Bell had been involved with a restaurant business in Whitefield, near Manchester. It was initially a partnership with the former Burnley centre-half Colin Waldron, but Bell finally sold his share in 1990 when he returned to Maine Road.

A conversation with Ken Barnes and Howard Kendall led to him coming back for two days a week to work with the youngsters. This job 'snowballed' into the one he has today – 'Half the time youth team development officer (with Terry Farrell), and the other half working with Neil McNab.

'I also do the odd bit of scouting for Jimmy Frizzell and take the Under-16 sides on a Sunday. I help with the YTS scheme and on Thursday evenings I run the school of excellence. Every day of the week I'm doing something for City. I'm convinced I was put on this earth to be involved with football. My playing days are long gone now so I do other things.'

Did he ever harbour thoughts of management? 'No, I couldn't be a manager. Even during my playing career I preferred never to be noticed off the pitch. I never liked being in the public eye.'

There is another game which brings back memories for Colin Bell – the championship decider at Newcastle in 1968. 'Nobody in my lifetime could have written the script for that day. The whole championship depended on the last two games of the season. The two Manchester clubs could win the league and they were playing two north-east clubs and I'm from the north-east.

'United had Sunderland (the team I followed as a boy), at Old Trafford. Sunderland were struggling and it looked like a certain home-win. We were at Newcastle – a place where we didn't usually get much. At half-time the scores were level at both grounds. We played really well in the second half and I managed to lay on a couple of goals for Neil Young and Francis Lee. As everyone knows, we won 4–3, but Sunderland surprised everyone by beating United.

'There were 46,000 people at St James's Park that day – they were even sitting on the running-track. The atmosphere was fantastic. Mind you, so many people since have told me they were there, I'm sure the crowd must have been double that!'

It was undoubtedly a great game for Manchester City – and for Colin Bell.

Monday, 26 December 1977

Football League Division One at Maine Road

Manchester City	4	(Tueart 3, Kidd)
Newcastle United	0	

MANCHESTER CITY	v.	NEWCASTLE UNITED
Joe Corrigan	1	Kevin Carr
Kenny Clements	2	Irving Nattrass
Willie Donachie	3	Mike Barker
Tommy Booth	4	Tommy Cassidy
Dave Watson	5	John Bird
*Paul Power	6	John Blackley*
Peter Barnes	7	Dennis Martin
Gary Owen	8	Terry Burns
Brian Kidd	9	Paul Cannell
Asa Hartford	10	Tommy Craig
Dennis Tueart	11	Stuart Robinson
*Colin Bell	SUB	Martin Gorry*

Attendance: 45,811

9

NIALL QUINN

City v. Derby County
Football League Division One at Maine Road, 20 April 1991

It is now more than six years since Niall Quinn joined City from Arsenal. During this time the 6ft 3ins Republic of Ireland centre-forward has played at both ends of the top division of English football. Unfortunately for Niall (and for everyone else connected with Manchester City), as far as cup finals go, the nearest he has been to Wembley was the quarter-final of the 1993–94 FA Cup.

City fans will remember that game. It was the day when Mike Sheron gave the Blues an early lead, Tottenham replied with four and then Terry Phelan scored a great goal after a run of fully 50 yards. It was also the day when the new Umbro Stand was opened and events were further spoiled by a pitch invasion.

So, with no cup final to choose as his idea of Blue Heaven, which game would Niall go for? The one I remembered in particular was at Crystal Palace on 1 April 1991 – just three days after Niall had scored against England at Wembley. City won 3–1 at Palace and Quinn scored all three – a tap-in, a volley and the third with his head. The perfect hat-trick against a team that was lying third in the First Division.

I had been wrong before with my ideas in advance of meeting the players, so it came as no surprise when I was wrong again. 'Derby County at Maine Road, in the same month as that Palace game,' Niall told me. 'They were exciting times. I think we were fourth in the First Division – remember, this was before the Premiership so it was the top division – and we had only lost one of our previous seven matches. It was really a great time and everybody at the club was buzzing.

'I remember Peter Shilton pulled out just before the game with an injury. We were all delighted with this because he was obviously a world-class goalkeeper, and had been to the World Cup in Italy the previous summer. We thought we might get something if we could test his young replacement, Martin Taylor, early on.'

This very nearly happened. Good play down the left by City involved Mark Brennan, Quinn himself and left-back Neil Pointon. Pointon's cross on the run was deflected into the path of the diving Quinn but unfortunately his header from the penalty spot was straight at Taylor.

In the 22nd minute City took the lead in a game Derby had to win to stand any chance of survival in the First Division. (It was perhaps not surprising that the Rams found themselves in this unenviable position. They had gone 19 matches without a win and had bought just one player in two and a half years.)

Steve Redmond's long free-kick from inside City's half was headed up in the air by Derby's number six, England youth international Jason Kavanagh. Quinn back-headed it to Ward who then returned it to Quinn over the head of Mark Wright. From the edge of the penalty area Quinn struck a low, left-foot volley into the corner of the net.

'I was quite pleased with that,' says Quinn modestly, 'but not long afterwards Tony Coton was being sent off and for a while nobody was really sure what was going on.'

This occurred just on the half-hour, when Derby were thrown a priceless lifeline. Brennan's ball aimed towards Quinn on the right wing was intercepted by Wright who knocked the ball forward to Pickering. He played a long ball over the City defence who had failed to move out together and played Dean Saunders onside.

One on one with Coton, the Welsh international took the ball to the goalkeeper's right and was brought down – an obvious penalty. City's only arguments were with the linesman concerning the offside, or rather, the lack of it.

Referee Ken Lupton of Stockton felt obliged to enforce the newly revised law to the letter and promptly showed Coton the red card.

Captain Steve Redmond led the protests but they were all in vain. 'Everyone started to look around and I said, "I'll go in goal",' Quinn recalls. 'As I was putting the jersey on I then thought "What am I doing?" I got a bit nervous when I thought about the penalty. I remember Tony throwing his gloves away in anger – one of them hit the referee – and then I picked them up and went in goal. I thought to myself, "I'll have a laugh here – I probably won't save it but I'll have a guess."'

It was Saunders himself who took the kick, low down and to the goalkeeper's left. 'I guessed the right way and kept it out. It was a situation where I had absolutely nothing to lose. I wasn't expected to save it and if it had gone in, nobody was going to give out to me.

'I've seen the save once or twice since on television and video but what disappoints me most is that they never show the resulting corner. I caught the ball on the edge of the box and in doing so knocked over Mark Wright and Mick Harford. Nobody ever remembers that! I then did a perfect drop-kick out to the left wing, to Mark Ward I think it was. That for me was better than saving the penalty but it's always forgotten.'

Player-manager Peter Reid later said, 'He does a bit of goalkeeping in training. He gives a tenner to anyone who can score three out of five penalties past him.'

A first half full of incident ended with Quinn's goal separating the sides. In the second half it was still City – despite being down to ten men – who continued to make the chances. Neil Pointon had the best of these when he beat the on-rushing Taylor only to see Mark Wright clear his shot off the line.

With 15 minutes left, Peter Reid brought himself on to replace Mark Ward. Ward was so angered with the decision that he refused to shake hands with Reid and then kicked over a bucket of water which splashed a policeman.

A minute later David White effectively sealed the game and consigned Derby to Second Division football. He intercepted Pickering's telegraphed cross-field ball before crashing an unstoppable left-foot shot high into the net from 15 yards. It was White's tenth league goal of the season and his second in consecutive games. His good run continued in the next game when he scored four times in an amazing 5–1 win at Villa Park. He would finish the season with 15 in the league, second place and six goals behind Niall Quinn. Not surprisingly, Quinn's goals earned him City's Player of the Year trophy for that 1990–91 season – a season in which he played in all 38 league games.

In the very last minute of the game Niall Quinn was finally beaten. His defence which had guarded him so well for an hour failed to pick up Mick Harford who scored with a header. But the goal came too late for Derby, both in this game and in the season.

Peter Gardner covered the Derby County game for the *Manchester Evening News*. His report stated:

> Manchester City have reached fourth place in the First Division after a six-game unbeaten run that has rewarded them with 14 points from a possible 18. That brief statistic was hidden behind the bizarre incidents of a stormy and controversial Maine Road match that ended with Derby County duly dispatched to the Second Division.
>
> The Blues can now confirm their arrival as one of the country's top four teams by squeezing Aston Villa a step nearer relegation tomorrow night. On current form City can take on anyone without fear . . . as they have proved in recent weeks with victories at Crystal Palace and Leeds, a draw at Arsenal plus a home victory over seven-goal Nottingham Forest, the FA Cup finalists.
>
> On the other hand, a desperate and dispirited Derby on Saturday were mere chicken feed for a side who even handicapped themselves to play for almost an hour with only ten men. The sending-off of goalkeeper Tony Coton enabled Niall Quinn to prove himself a folk hero in both penalty areas, with a goal at one end and a spot-kick save at the other as the high drama peaked.
>
> The storm did not blow out there, either. Petulant Mark Ward refused a handshake from his boss Peter Reid when substituted and kicked over a bucket of water that splashed over a policeman, to leave himself facing a £1,000 club fine.
>
> And they say nothing much happens at Maine Road these days!
>
> But back to the football. A 2–1 margin cannot adequately equate to the complete difference between a couple of teams who are clearly heading in different directions. Derby looked wretchedly ill-equipped for the task facing them from the outset,

and the only genuine surprise was that City did not score before Quinn's 22nd minute strike when he half-volleyed a splendid low shot teed up for him by Ward's header.

All hope for County then evaporated when Quinn went into goal to save the penalty from Dean Saunders, the man dragged down by Coton for the professional-foul sending-off of the City goalkeeper, who compounded his offence by recklessly hurling his gloves at referee Ken Lupton.

Derby even handed City their second goal on a plate, Nick Pickering giving the ball away to David White who danced by two more equally bemused defenders before finishing with a fine angled effort from the left. Mick Harford's last-minute headed goal was scant consolation for Derby who, the penalty apart, had rarely put in a serious shot to test Quinn, so ineffective were they on the day.

There was no doubting Quinn's right to man-of-the-match honours, yet tribute must also go to Andy Hill for another splendid display that provided further evidence of his continuing maturity in the First Division. The presence of Mark Brennan in front of Neil Pointon on the left also continues to provide the balance so necessary in any successful side.

With three games remaining, there is every reason to believe City can now maintain their current standing to finish in their highest position since 1978, when they were also fourth.

It wasn't just soccer that the young Niall Quinn was good at. 'Aye, there were other sports I wasn't bad at,' he recalls modestly. 'I played Gaelic football for Dublin Schoolboys and we went out to Australia to see if we could blend the game with Australian Rules. We were the first side to tour out there so I suppose we were the guinea pigs. We didn't do too badly; we lost the first four games, drew the fifth and then won our last four. Once we'd got used to their rules we got quite good at it.

'I had a chance to stay in Australia because two sides asked me to turn professional. I probably would have done so – six figure salaries were rumoured – but Arsenal came in for me when I came home.

'Soccer really was at the back of my mind at this time. Although I'd played regularly at school I wasn't attached to any major soccer club.

I was also doing a bit of hurling. I played for Dublin Minors in the 1983 All-Ireland Hurling Minor final after I came back from Australia and I never thought then that I'd be a professional soccer player.

'About a week after that hurling final, Arsenal's Irish scout Bill Darby came up to me. He said he'd been watching me for quite a while but didn't want to say anything to me until the hurling was out of the way.

'He asked me to go over to London for a trial period. Although I hadn't played any soccer for two and a half to three months I thought to myself, "Why not? You never know." Seven days into my two-weeks trial period they offered me a three-year contract. That was in November 1983.'

In December 1985 Quinn made his debut in the Arsenal first team. 'I don't remember too much about it really. It was against Liverpool at Highbury. Tony Woodcock was injured and I got my chance. I remember Bruce Grobbelaar throwing one out to me. He mistimed a shot from Paul Davis. I was about nine and a half stone at the time – despite being the same height as I am now – and I went hurtling in and forced the ball into the back of the net. Charlie Nicholas added a second and we ended up winning 2–0. The club had been going through a bad spell so it was a really good win for us.'

Quinn led the Arsenal attack in 35 of the 42 league games of the 1986–87 season. Over the next two and a half seasons, though, he made just 14 starts.

'I suppose I fell out of favour a little bit. I'd had a good long run and then suddenly I found myself out of the team. I kept battling away, got back in occasionally and scored a few times in the year Arsenal won the championship.

'I wasn't completely out of it, although at times I have to admit I felt it. George Graham put me on the bench a few times which did keep me involved a little, although obviously I'd have preferred to have been playing. The hardest times were when I didn't even travel with the first team. I would be playing a reserve game at an empty Highbury on a Saturday afternoon when the first team had gone up to, say, Leeds or Everton. I have to say those days weren't very enjoyable!'

In January 1990 Arsenal beat Stoke City 1–0 in an FA Cup tie. This proved to be Quinn's last goal for Arsenal as well as his last game in a Gunners' shirt. On 15 March he joined City for a fee of £800,000.

'Twenty minutes after meeting Howard Kendall I signed for City. I had no hesitation.

'Howard had taken over from Mel Machin that same season and had brought in several former Everton players. Because of the situation City were in he wanted players around him who had done things for him before and who knew what was expected of them. He stuck with what he knew and it worked. He kept the club up comfortably in the end and the following season we finished fifth.

'I have to say it was a huge turning point in City's fortunes when Howard Kendall was allowed to leave. You can go on and on about what's happened here since but I think it was a terrible mistake by the club to let him go. That clause in his contract was an awful pity and I don't think Howard was the same manager when he went back to Goodison Park. Things are different when you go back to your old club, and I'm sure City suffered because of his leaving.

'He'd had such success first time at Everton and everybody was thinking he would just carry on as he'd left off. It was always going to be difficult for him. City were an up-and-coming side and I'm sure we could have gone places.

'I used to score a lot more goals in those days. David White was great for me, as was Adrian Heath. He was a very clever player who hardly got any credit. He made a lot of space for people and caused mayhem in other teams' defences. It was unfair really, because while I was getting all the goals the crowd were giving Adrian a hard time.'

In the summer of 1986 Niall Quinn represented his country for the first time. Four years later came the pinnacle of any professional footballer's career – the World Cup finals. What are Quinn's recollections of Italia '90? 'For the whole build-up and perhaps the first two weeks of the tournament, David O'Leary and myself weren't really involved. We roomed together and spent most of the time training and picking the cones up!

'All of a sudden the team had a loss of form. We played poorly against Egypt and then Jack picked me instead of Tony Cascarino for the next game against Holland. It was amazing, really. I'd gone from hoping to get on for five minutes to playing against one of the best teams in the world. They had players like Van Basten, Rijkaard and Gullit – it was a fabulous side. Then just to cap it all I scored the equaliser which put us through to the next round.

'In that next round David scored the winning penalty and the whole atmosphere in our room changed completely. It went from not being involved at all to being a large part of everything that was going on. The penalty takers weren't decided in advance. I was suffering badly with cramp towards the end of the game and was just grateful I wasn't asked. I didn't fancy it at all!'

Was that memorable game against Romania in Genoa the greatest moment of Quinn's international career? 'No, it wasn't. I would say that scoring at Wembley against England in the European Championships was. We should have won that game. We outplayed England on the night and I think that was the best performance by any Irish side I've played in. Graham Taylor had a serious side out that night – he had Bryan Robson, David Platt, Peter Beardsley and Gary Lineker playing – and although the game finished 1–1 we murdered them.

'I wasn't really disappointed about missing the 1994 finals simply because I'd had plenty of time to get used to it. I got injured at Sheffield Wednesday the previous November so I knew for months that I wasn't going to make it. I had exactly the same injury as Paul Lake, the only difference being that my operation turned out better than his did. It is a tragedy to think that his footballing career is over.'

Niall Quinn – a player who insists on getting 12 hours' sleep on the night before a game – is the only player still at Maine Road today who played in that game against Derby County. Neil Pointon and Steve Redmond moved to nearby Oldham Athletic and David White to Leeds. Colin Hendry won a Premier League championship medal with Blackburn Rovers and the dismissed goalkeeper Tony Coton joined Manchester United in somewhat controversial circumstances during the 1995–96 season.

Quinn has other recollections of the game: 'I remember someone passed the ball back to me when I was in goal and I flicked it up and then cleared it. I looked across to the bench where Peter Reid was sitting shaking his head. I think I'd stretched his nerves to the limit, but by this time the adrenalin was flowing and I was enjoying myself. I felt I could do anything that day.

'They pulled a goal back in the last minute. Steve Redmond ducked when he could have headed the ball away and I came out to catch it.

Unfortunately Mick Harford nipped in and headed it past me. I was stranded in no man's land and there was really nothing I could do about it.

'Funnily enough that was the one and only time I've ever played in goal in a competitive game. I mess around sometimes in training and I suppose there's an unwritten law nowadays that if there were three outplayers on the bench then I would be the standby keeper. I don't mind that – in fact I quite like the idea!

'The last day of that season we played Sunderland at Maine Road. Like Derby, they too needed to win to stay in the First Division. There was a big crowd; I remember they brought thousands of fans with them. In the end we won the game 3–2 and sent Sunderland down as well. I scored twice that day – David White got the other – so I suppose Manchester City and Niall Quinn in particular weren't very popular at the time in either the Midlands or the North-East!'

Known on local radio as 'The Big Irishman', Niall Quinn scored on his debut for City in a 1–1 Maine Road draw against Chelsea on 21 March 1990. Shortly after that game he moved to Altrincham, where he still lives, joined today by his wife Gillian and their young daughter Aisling. In these recent troublesome times he has been the subject of much transfer speculation, with clubs ranging from Sporting Lisbon to Sheffield United (managed by Howard Kendall) being among those showing interest. Throughout all these stories one thing has remained constant – Niall Quinn's loyalty to Manchester City Football Club.

A player who always gives 100 per cent in every game, Quinn found himself battling for his striker's position with Paul Walsh, Uwe Rösler and, most recently, Georgian international Mikhail Kavelashvili. Noted throughout the country as one of the best headers of the ball over the years Quinn has also worked hard at his ground techniques and now shows considerable skill and deftness for such a big man. This work was acknowledged in 1995 with the limited edition 'Quinninho' T-shirt.

Unfortunately the T-shirt was in the shops at the same time as City made their worst ever start to a season, with a run of defeats that kept the Blues in the relegation zone for most of the campaign. A win was needed in the last game against Liverpool. A 2–2 draw ensued and City were relegated.

Not surprisingly, it was a desperately upset Niall Quinn who spoke to *Match of the Day*'s Tony Gubba after that game: 'There's a huge cloud over the club. As a player – and on behalf of the rest of the players – I can only apologise. Not for today's performance, or for the last couple of performances, but for perhaps the way we started the year and the problems we placed upon the club. As one of the team I can just apologise to those who have travelled the length and breadth of the country following us. At the end of the day the buck stops with us.

'Our form in recent games counts for nothing now. The feeling amongst all the players including myself is that you look back to your careers, you look back when you started and you go to big clubs on trials. You think football is the greatest thing in the world. You get accepted at a club and you're the bee's knees. Everyone is happy for you. Nobody ever told me there'd be days like this. It's a bit hard to swallow.'

His final words on the matter were as follows: 'Without doubt the club was let down badly by the players last season. I feel so sorry for the fans who have supported us so magnificently. My only wish now is to be part of a City side which bounces straight back into the Premiership – the only division Manchester City should be in.'

Everybody is right behind you, Niall.

Saturday, 20 April 1991

Football League Division One at Maine Road

Manchester City	2	(Quinn, White)
Derby County	1	(Harford)

MANCHESTER CITY	v.	DERBY COUNTY
Tony Coton	1	Martin Taylor
Andy Hill	2	Melvyn Sage
Neil Pointon	3	Nick Pickering
Adrian Heath	4	Geraint Williams
Colin Hendry	5	Mark Wright
Steve Redmond	6	Jason Kavanagh**
David White	7	Garry Micklewhite
Mark Brennan	8	Dean Saunders
Niall Quinn	9	Mick Harford
Alan Harper	10	Ian Wilson*
*Mark Ward	11	Paul Williams
*Peter Reid	SUB	Mark Patterson*
Clive Allen	SUB	Stephen Cross**

Attendance: 24,037

10

ASA HARTFORD

City v. Manchester United
Football League Cup Fourth Round at Maine Road,
12 November 1975

'If he's got a hole in the heart, then there's something wrong with all of us.' These were the comments of former City chief scout Ken Barnes shortly before Asa Hartford joined the Blues in the summer of 1974; comments that were echoed by Tony Book during his reminiscences for this book.

The story had started two years earlier. 'It was difficult to take in at the time,' recalls Hartford today. 'I'd just turned 21 – literally a few days before – and I'd had the medical at Leeds. Don Revie then sat me down and told me I'd probably need heart surgery.

'It just didn't seem right. I was playing at West Bromwich where Don Howe was manager. Don was a bit of a taskmaster. He was an excellent coach; he knew his stuff and worked the players hard. We used to do a lot of cross-country running and with me being one of the younger players I was normally up with the front runners. I always thought people with bad hearts would get out of breath even walking upstairs, so the fact that I was a good runner never gave me cause to think I had a problem. The whole thing just didn't add up.

'At The Hawthorns we just had general medical check-ups. At Leeds it was different; they put me on an ECG and that's where an abnormality showed up. That was on a Friday afternoon and on the

131

Saturday they took me to hospital for further tests. The tests there confirmed what they'd found at Leeds – there was an abnormality.

'When I went back to West Bromwich they sent me to a specialist in Birmingham for some specific tests to see if I could still carry on as a footballer.' (It should be pointed out here that when these tests were carried out, Hartford was a Scottish Under-21 international and had played for five years at The Hawthorns).

'When you see any medical people they always err on the side of caution. Remember, he was putting his reputation on the line, but he said everything was okay and there was nothing to worry about. I wish I'd never known anything about it, but I suppose it was just one of those things. To this day I have regular check-ups and, touch wood, I've never had any trouble with it.

'Leeds were about to fork out a lot of money and I think it was the word "abnormality" that forced them to pull out. Even to this day, though, I sometimes think back to that conversation with Don Revie. I couldn't understand it then and I still can't understand it 20-odd years later.' Abnormality or not, on 13 August 1974, Asa Hartford arrived at Maine Road for a fee of £210,000. His debut came four days later in a 4–0 home win against West Ham United in the opening game of the 1974–75 season. 'I don't remember too much about that game to be honest,' he admits, 'but I do remember the next one. We beat Tottenham 1–0 on the Wednesday. I remember that because I got the goal that day – which was unusual for me!

'Pat Jennings was in goal for Spurs and after the game he came over and congratulated me. That made me feel good, and gave me a bit of confidence. I wasn't exactly in awe of the place, but I had come from a small club to a big club. City still had Mike Summerbee, Colin Bell and Denis Law who'd just come back from the World Cup in Germany, although my City playing career with Francis Lee lasted just 24 hours. He moved to Derby County the day after I arrived at Maine Road!'

Asa Hartford is one of only a handful of players who've enjoyed two spells at Maine Road. His most memorable City game came during his first. 'Against United in the League Cup on 12 November 1975.

'The thing that everyone remembers about that game is the injury to Colin Bell. I was right behind Colin when it happened and although we knew it was bad, we didn't know just how bad at the time. It was a few days later before the full extent of the injury was known.

'The game itself stuck in my mind because it's one of the few I've ever played in when almost everything I tried came off. I wouldn't say it was perfect but it was certainly very enjoyable for me.' Apart from Bell's injury, the game was certainly enjoyable for City fans as well!

Straight from the kick-off Peter Barnes was obstructed by United's Canadian-born right-back Jimmy Nichol. Alan Oakes took the free-kick from wide out on the left wing and hoisted the ball high into the United penalty area. Dave Watson's header began an enormous scramble, which ended only when Dennis Tueart shot high into the net. City were a goal up after just 35 seconds. 'That was a tremendous start,' Hartford recalls. 'It really fired everybody up.'

Less than five minutes later Colin Bell suffered that horrific injury – an injury that was thought initially would keep him out for a month. It actually kept him out of City's first team for more than two years.

Tommy Booth came on as replacement for Bell and had been in the action for just nine minutes when Hartford extended City's lead. 'Yes, I remember that. Again it started with a cross from the left – Willie Donachie this time – and Joe Royle nodded it down for me. I managed to get to the ball just before Paddy Roche and lifted it over him from about eight yards.

'In a way I suppose it was a bit like the winning goal in the League Cup final the following year. Again Willie crossed from the left and Tommy Booth knocked it back for Dennis Tueart to score. It wasn't something that we worked on particularly in training. All we did was use Willie's natural ability to cross the ball, and made sure there was support in the box. In that United game we had Peter Barnes wide on the left and Dennis Tueart wide on the right. As a midfield player it was great for me – I always had options open.'

Tueart put the game beyond United's reach in the 28th minute. Forsaking his wide position, he picked the ball up in the centre-circle, just inside his own half. In a style reminiscent of a greyhound in the final hundred yards, Tueart simply ran as fast as he could, straight at the already-shell-shocked United defence. From just outside the box he crashed an unstoppable shot past Roche's left hand and into the corner of the net. 'Dennis was a very direct player,' remembers

Hartford. 'A lot of people used to think he was an out-and-out winger but he was also comfortable playing up front or dropping off slightly behind the front line. He could play in any position up front. That's the mark of a good player.

'He was also one of the best volleyers I've ever seen. I played with a fellow called Tony Brown at West Bromwich and he was a great volleyer too but Dennis was right up there with him. You knew that if either Dennis or Colin Bell was going to have a shot, then it was a fair bet it was going to be on target. All right, they might miss with the odd one or two but you could never say that about me. With me it could be high or wide or both – they could have gone anywhere!'

A standing ovation greeted the half-time whistle. The vulnerability of United's defence was once again on show, as it had been for most of their earlier games. All season their problem had not been scoring goals; in fact simply the opposite was true. However, apart from a goal-line clearance by Oakes from Stuart Pearson's effort, United had never looked like scoring in the first half. To be fair, though, it should be said that it is virtually impossible to score when the ball is constantly in your half of the pitch!

City's overwhelming superiority continued throughout the second half, and with just 12 minutes to go their lead was increased. Four rampaging blue shirts were homing in on four retreating red ones as Donachie's pass found Barnes out on the left. With his trusty left foot the 18 year-old winger fired a low cross into the penalty area which was converted by a sliding Joe Royle. The speed and simplicity of that goal typified the whole evening.

'Another one from the left. I remember that goal – it was a good finish by Joe. I was at a dinner earlier this year organised by Dennis Tueart and they showed the goal on video. Super finish; he caught it on the half-volley on his way in. Joe was a great target man and I always loved playing when there was that kind of player in the side. You look at Chelsea's Mark Hughes today. He does a similiar kind of job to Joe, holding the ball so people can catch the attack up.'

Rarely, either before or since, have newspapers been so glowing in their reports of City as they were in the days following that marvellous 4–0 victory. Praise was heaped on every City player – but one in particular received more than the others. That one was Asa Hartford.

According to *The Guardian,*

> Bell's injury seemed to inspire City. It certainly inspired Asa
> Hartford who thereafter played with stunning brilliance. He has
> not always played to his capabilities but last night he was faultless
> and scored a goal with a piece of fierce finishing. He sent in some
> thunderous drives that were not far off target. But the outstanding
> aspects of his performance were his imagination, the accuracy and
> inventiveness of his passing and the eagerness of his running. It
> was his probing more than anything else which exposed the
> weaknesses at the heart of the United defence.

'It was just one of those games for me,' recalls Hartford modestly.
'Balls would come down and, almost without looking, I was volleying
them to a blue shirt. It seemed as though I could do no wrong that night!

'To be honest, I didn't realise we'd scored our first goal so early. In
a derby game that is a great fillip and it gave everybody a tremendous
boost. In a way, perhaps Colin's injury galvanised everyone. One of
our best players was carried off and the rest of us thought we were
really going to have to get together.

'Tommy Booth was a very good player, and although he did play
quite a few games in midfield you could never honestly say he was a
genuine midfielder. Colin was our engine-room. He could get up and
down the pitch so easily. Any side would miss a player like that.'

In the next day's *Guardian* Paul Fitzpatrick described the game for
those who were unfortunate not to have witnessed the events either at
first hand or on television. Or maybe he described events for those
who had seen the game and already wanted to relive it. Whatever the
reason, it was a fine example of football writing:

> When things have gone wrong for Manchester United this season
> Tommy Docherty, the club's manager, has usually dismissed
> disappointment by saying that it has all been good experience for
> his young players. But last night at Maine Road in the fourth
> round Football League Cup tie, Docherty's young lions suffered
> something more than mere disappointment. They endured a
> bruising experience that could remain with impressionable minds
> for a long time.

The character of United's youngsters must now be on trial.
How quickly can they recover from such an experience? They
were torn apart by a Manchester City side playing football of
classical dimensions – fluent, imaginative, decisive, at times
breathtaking – and it will need some expert psychology on
Docherty's part to convince his men that the end of the world has
still not arrived.

For most of this season United have attacked opponents with
non-stop energy. The policy has worked. They have won points
and games, and have treated big crowds everywhere to some
outstanding football. But doubts about United's defence have
persisted, and last night those doubts were confirmed. United
were subject to intense pressure, and were simply not able to cope
with it.

Their goalkeeper, Roche, had a traumatic night, and the men
in front of him were as lacking in confidence. Houston time and
time again was beaten by the pace of Tueart or the precocious
Barnes; Nicholl, promising though he undoubtedly is, betrayed
his inexperience; Greenhoff repeatedly was caught out of position
or beaten in the air; and even the usually impeccable Buchan was
surprisingly vulnerable.

But whatever United's faults – and all City's goals originated in
error – there was no denying the quality of City's football. Almost
everyone was agreed that it was by far their best performance of
the season. Others considered it City's finest display for years. I
would go along with the latter view. It was, to use a word in
current football vogue, magic.

It was all achieved without the services of Marsh, that talented
but enigmatic character, who now appears destined for foreign
shores. And it was achieved without the considerable services of
Bell, who played outstandingly in City's last match with
Birmingham City. Bell was carried off on a stretcher after only five
minutes, the victim of a high tackle by Buchan. Bell tore a muscle
at the back of a thigh, and will be out of the game for a month.
[This, of course, was not to be the case.] He will, therefore, miss
England's crucial European Championship game with Portugal.

City's performance, had Bell remained in their ranks, would
have been commendable enough. Without him it was little short

of miraculous, for City had to substitute a defender – Booth – although he played a big part in City's victory. Indeed, no one played below par, and even Corrigan, on the few times that he was tested, looked unbeatable.

If Hartford is singled out for special praise, it was difficult to fault a single City player. From Corrigan, who made one outstanding save from McIlroy in the second half, to the talented Barnes, City bristled with class and flair. Tueart can rarely have run with greater pace or purpose; Barnes is probably the most exciting young player to emerge since George Best; and if the City supporters sometimes allowed themselves a joke at the leaden-footed ball control of Royle, let them. He has had his trials, but is proving his worth.

Having to concentrate so much on defence, it was not surprising that the United forwards were given little opportunity to show their ability. On one occasion a shot from Pearson seemed destined for a corner of the net, but the indestructible Oakes appeared from seemingly nowhere to clear off the line. Had Pearson scored at that still early stage the tale might have been different. He did not and but for brief interludes, United were put on the rack and stretched to breaking point by the speed and precision of City's football. City capitalised on a perfect start, which saw them take the lead after 35 seconds. Nicholl, who has unhappy memories of his last derby match when he scored an own goal, obstructed the swift-running Barnes, and Oakes took the kick. Watson outjumped the statuesque United defence and nodded the ball forward. There followed an unsightly scramble before Tueart, who had already had one stab at the ball, shot high into the net. United's defence had two opportunities to clear the ball and failed each time. It was the beginning of their ceaseless misery.

Bell's departure soon afterwards could have been deflating, but City reorganised were no mean force. And in the 14th minute they went further ahead. Again United's defence was beaten in the air, this time by Royle, who nodded Donachie's centre into the path of the in-rushing Hartford. There was nothing that Roche could do about the resultant, ferocious, left-foot shot.

Could United retrieve something from the wreckage? The answer was quickly forthcoming. They could not, and in the 28th minute Tueart scored his second goal – one which put the contest out of United's already faltering reach. This time the normally impeccable Buchan lost possession five yards inside the City half. Tueart was away like a hare. His run was a long one, but there was no stopping him or his shot. Roche had been left cruelly exposed, but was slow to leave his goal.

Not surprisingly, City went in at half-time to a rapturous ovation, and although they scored only one goal in the second half, their football was if anything even better than it had been in the first. And in the 78th minute City confirmed their authority beyond all doubt. Nicholl lost possesion, and there followed a sweeping movement between Tueart, Donachie, and Barnes before Royle imperiously swept the ball home from close range. It was a perfect end.

This was City's 11th game without defeat, and without doubt provided vindication of the sacking by Tony Book of his wayward genius, Marsh. Who needs the unpredictable skills of Marsh when City can achieve heights like this without him?

Hartford scored again in the next round, a 4–2 home win against Third Division Mansfield Town. He finished the season with 12 goals in all competitions, missing just three games along the way. 'I probably missed those through suspension,' he quipped. 'Most of the games I missed throughout my career were because of suspension. I hardly ever had a really serious injury. I had the occasional muscle strain, but on the whole I was very lucky.'

Dennis Tueart's name again cropped up in the conversation. 'I always liked to come out on the field at the back of the team. It was a little superstition of mine – and it was also one of Dennis's. We'd usually jockey for position; sometimes I'd be last and he'd be second and then the next time it would be the other way around. Another one of my superstitions was to put my left sock and left boot on first, but I don't think that's exclusive to me!

'The City sides of that period were a fine mixture of experience and youth. We had the older heads such as Joe Corrigan, Colin Bell and Joe Royle but we had some great youngsters as well. Players such as Peter Barnes – who had a really good game against United and then went on to score at Wembley – Gary Owen and Paul Power. I don't think Paul Power was given enough credit for what he did at City. He was a real grafter. Nowadays I think he'd be outstanding. He'd be called a wing-back today and I will always remember the countless times he sprinted up and down the left wing. On a humorous note, Paul used to wear contact lenses and the players called him "Magoo". At some grounds where the floodlights weren't perfect, he would get dazzled and couldn't see the ball!'

In June 1979, after more than 200 games in five seasons, Asa Hartford found himself on Malcolm Allison's list of unwanted players. He moved to Nottingham Forest for £400,000. 'Only a short stay – I played three games in a couple of months, then I joined Everton. I had two years at Goodison and then John Bond brought me back to Maine Road in October 1981.

'I made my second debut in a League Cup tie against Stoke at Maine Road. We won 2–0 – I scored – and then lost 2–0 there in the return leg. We won the tie in the end 9–8 on penalties but I missed mine! In between we'd played Manchester United, Arsenal and Nottingham Forest in the league so it was quite a welcome back.

'Because of an ankle injury I missed a lot of the 1983–84 season. I don't think Billy McNeill fancied me really, and at the end of the season he released me. I went across to the States to Fort Lauderdale, purely to get myself fit again. I played about 30 games out there with Dave Watson, who'd left a fortnight or so before me, and the Peruvian World Cup star Cubillas.

'When I came back to England I joined Norwich City and we won the League Cup that season, when my shot was deflected and we beat Sunderland 1–0 in the final. The big disappointment then was the fact we couldn't play in Europe because of the Heysel tragedy.'

In July that year Hartford moved back up north to Bolton. He was now 34. 'Unlike other players, I never thought one bit about what I was going to do when I stopped playing. I just wanted to carry on. I remember that Ken Barnes once said to me, "Just keep on playing for as long as you can. They are the best days of your life." I always carried that thought around with me.

'After Bolton I moved to Stockport for a while as player-manager, and it was probably around this time that I thought I might like to get into coaching. I enjoyed it at Stockport but it was hard work. There was no money but it was great experience.'

Shrewsbury was the next step on 'Hartford's Tour'. 'I went there as player-coach and then Ian McNeill the manager lost his job and I became player-manager. In January 1991, after just 12 months, they parted company with me as well and so I tried my luck with Boston United. I had a good time there even though I had turned 40. I played about 12 or 15 times in the Vauxhall Conference. I stayed until May and was then offered the reserve team job at Blackburn Rovers.' How did that come about – who did he know? 'Nobody really – it was quite strange. I was doing a bit of scouting for Ian McNeill my former boss at Shrewsbury, who had gone to Millwall as assistant to Bruce Rioch. I was watching a play-off game at Burnden Park – I think it was Bolton versus Bury – and the place was packed. In the seat to my right was John Beck, the ex-Preston manager, and to my left was Sammy Chung, the former Wolves boss.

'At half-time we were just chatting away and Sammy said to me "What are you doing at the moment?" I said, "Nothing much," to which he replied "Right, my gaffer might be looking for someone to take the reserve side. Give me your number and I'll give you a call." At the time I didn't know which club Sammy was talking about. I had no idea where he was working. It turned out he was chief scout at Blackburn where Don McKay was manager. Sammy rang me a couple of weeks later, and I went for an interview and got the job.

'It was amazing, really. If I hadn't gone to that game, or if I'd sat two rows further back – I would never have had that conversation with Sammy. Kenny Dalglish came in shortly afterwards and the club just took off.

'During all these moves, I'd kept the house I had lived in during my playing days at Maine Road so I was used to all the travelling. I spent two years with Kenny before moving to Stoke City, first with Joe Jordan and then with Lou Macari. In July 1995 I was doing pre-season with Stoke when Francis Lee and Alan Ball got in touch and offered me the job here. I think Stoke had reported back earlier than City because I seem to remember I arrived at Maine Road about five days before the players!

'Once I got the offer I had no hesitation – it's a fantastic job. The set-up here is magnificent and I'm sure it won't be too long before the club is back where it belongs.'

Wednesday, 12 November 1975

Football League Cup Fourth Round at Maine Road

Manchester City	4	(Tueart 2, Hartford, Royle)
Manchester United	0	

MANCHESTER CITY	v.	MANCHESTER UNITED
Joe Corrigan	1	Paddy Roche
Kenny Clements	2	Jimmy Nichol
Willie Donachie	3	Stewart Houston
Mike Doyle	4	Tommy Jackson*
Dave Watson	5	Brian Greenhoff
Alan Oakes	6	Martin Buchan
Peter Barnes	7	Steve Coppell
*Colin Bell	8	Sammy McIlroy
Joe Royle	9	Stuart Pearson
Asa Hartford	10	Lou Macari
Dennis Tueart	11	Gerry Daly
*Tommy Booth	SUB	David McCreery*

Attendance: 50,182

11

ROY CLARKE

City v. Sunderland
FA Cup semi-final at Villa Park, 26 March 1955

Royston James Clarke was born in Newport on 1 June 1925 and as a schoolboy in South Wales excelled at sports. He was good enough to swim at county level, a feat he also achieved in diving, and played rugby regularly until the age of 11. It was then that the scrum-half Clarke had his front teeth kicked out by Reg Blakemore, a player who would eventually become a hooker with St Helens. This, understandably, was the end of Clarke's short career as a rugby player.

Money was scarce in Wales during those years between the wars, and as a result schools could not afford the expensive equipment required to play organised cricket in the summer months. An anglicised version of baseball took its place, with the only expense being a bat, a ball and four base markers. The great British weather would also prove less of an inconvenience. Such was the popularity of baseball in Wales that amateur leagues were established in and around Newport and Cardiff, and large crowds would gather to watch games on the local parks. Not surprisingly the sports-mad Clarke took to this game immediately, and would later prove good enough to represent his beloved country. Even today he still has his Welsh international schoolboy baseball jersey, bright red and resplendent with the three white feathers. He also claims to be the undisputed table tennis champion of Manchester City Football Club.

Fortunately for City, whilst all these other sporting activities were taking place, Clarke still loved, and was very good at, football. He joined Cardiff City as a junior in December 1942, and scored 11 times in 39 league games before a £12,000 move to Maine Road on 23 May 1947.

Eight years later in 1955, Len Shackleton, soccer's great 'Clown Prince' of the era, published his autobiography. There is a famous chapter in the book entitled 'The Average Director's Knowledge of Football'. This page is deliberately blank! Shackleton played nearly 400 league games (as well as five times for England) in a career spanning 11 years, and featured in several matches for Sunderland against Roy Clarke's City. Roy particularly remembers two of these clashes when asked to recall his most memorable match.

'It's a difficult decision to make, between two games against the same team. The first was at Maine Road on 6 September 1947 and we won 3–0. I scored that day. I picked up the ball in the inside-left position on the half-way line, running towards the old Platt Lane stand. Coming out of the centre-circle with the ball, I remember Len Shackleton coming across to tackle me and I beat him. I pushed the ball slightly to the left and I hit it. Shut my eyes and hit it, actually, and it went like a rocket into the back of the net. The referee blew his whistle and there it was, half-time. At first it wasn't accepted as a goal – the whistle just seemed to take the edge off it.' Clarke also remembers Shackleton walking up to him, patting him on the head and saying 'Well done, son'. Shackleton was a player Clarke admired greatly, saying he had the personal skill of players like Rodney Marsh and Georgiou Kinkladze.

The second clash with Sunderland, and one perhaps the fans will remember more vividly, was the 1955 FA Cup semi-final in the mud bath of Villa Park. The game was played on 26 March, the same day that Quare Times won the Grand National, and the newspaper unions began strike action when their demand for a pay rise of £2 18s 6d was rejected!

City had arrived at Villa Park by way of Derby County, Manchester United, Luton Town (where Clarke had scored two goals), and, in the sixth round, Birmingham City. Such was the severity of the rain at

Villa Park on the day, the match was still in doubt just 30 minutes before the 3 p.m. kick-off. At that time the Chief Constable of Birmingham came into the changing-rooms and told the referee the game had to be played. He was worried about the traffic problem – a crowd of 58,498 was already in the ground – and also about a possible fixture pile-up at Villa Park over the next few weeks.

Clarke remembers having sympathy for the supporters that day. 'They were wringing wet before the match, during the match and after the match. We players were only wet for 90 minutes.'

Minutes into the game conditions were appalling. It was virtually impossible to pass the ball along the ground. The only way was to play the ball in the air, and once again Clarke remembers the great Len Shackleton: 'He would flick the ball up, bounce it on his knee and then volley his passes.' Shackleton would perform these volleys regularly and was extremely accurate over great distances.

City eventually won the game 1–0, the winning goal being scored by number 11 Roy Clarke. Over 40 years later he still remembers the moment clearly. 'We scored in the second half from a centre by Joe Hayes. It was a free-kick out on the right, aimed towards inside-left Bob Johnstone. I was in the outside-left position at the back of the box so I saw everything. Well, Bob's only five foot nothing, and as the ball was coming across, I knew he would miss it. It was just a feeling I had. I thought if Bob misses it, I'm in with a chance. Long before the ball reached Bob I dived towards it. It just dropped over Bob's head as he tried to reach it, so I headed it – with quite a pace – towards the right-hand side of the goal, to the left of goalkeeper Willie Fraser. The ball hit the net and slowly rolled back out and into play.

'A photograph was taken at this precise moment and not one person in the crowd shows any movement or expression that a goal has been scored. It seemed to take a few seconds for anyone to realise what had happened. It was almost in slow motion.'

The state of the ground that day placed more emphasis on the physical attributes of the players rather than their skill. Clarke recalls the presence of Bert Trautmann in goal as being a tremendous influence, knowing full well the German's capabilities behind the defence. Despite Sunderland being the more-fancied side (they would finish the season in fourth place against City's seventh), and having the enigmatic Shackleton, City, in Clarke's own words, 'deserved to win'.

145

'We had a good defence,' he added. 'We had players who worked hard. We had strong players, like Dave Ewing, Roy Paul and Jimmy Meadows, as well as skilful players like Ken Barnes and again, Roy Paul. He was good at everything as well as being captain.

'I remember getting tackled by a Sunderland player as I came back to pick up a loose ball. In the collision he fell awkwardly across my knee and I've had problems with it ever since. Roy Paul walked across to me, lifted me up and carried me off the pitch. This was with three minutes to go and it was the end of the game for me.'

At this point Clarke also remembers some unprintable comments 'from one Welshman to another', and admits to some 1950s professionalism: 'Before the injury I collapsed deep inside their half, right up near the corner flag. I was chasing a ball and everyone thought I had just run myself into the ground, that I was absolutely physically gone. Little did they know that I was play-acting just to waste time after I'd scored, and I was trying to gain a free-kick. The full-back came across with a sliding tackle and I just dived. Not like they dive nowadays. In those days when you got kicked up in the air you never bothered about it. You just got on with the game.'

The match took place in the days long before the players' lounge was a fixture at football stadiums. Friends or relatives waiting for players after the games would have to wait outside the grounds, and the 1955 FA Cup semi-final was no exception. Clarke remembers, 'When I came out of the ground, my mother and father were waiting for me. My mother walked straight past me and began to walk into the ground. I turned to my father and asked where she was going. Armed with her umbrella, she was going to have a word with the Sunderland full-back.'

Fortunately Clarkes senior and junior managed to persuade the enraged Mrs Clarke otherwise, therefore preventing a potentially controversial incident. Imagine the tabloid press of the 1990s with a story like that!

Clarke's parents had been loyal supporters of Roy's since his early playing days and were particularly proud when he was asked to play for Lovell's Athletic during the wartime FA Cup. As a large sweet producing company, Lovell's found themselves in the enviable and lucrative position of being able to pay players to turn out for the company side. This was a great honour at the time (as well as being beneficial to the player's pocket), as players were allowed to guest for other teams during the war so long as it was cleared in advance with your own side.

Cardiff City were Clarke's club at the time, and they gave Roy permission to play for Lovell's in both legs of an FA Cup tie with Bath City. Guesting for Bath at the time was future Blackpool and England centre-forward Stan Mortenson. The Lovell's factory was in Newport, just about 100 yards from where Clarke was born, and he recalls his mum and dad bragging and boasting to everyone about 'their boy' on the train journey to Bath. The irony of the situation was that everyone on the train was a football person, be it player, official or reporter, and knew exactly who 'their boy' was. The obvious bursting pride of Clarke's parents was not damaged, though, as not one single person acknowledged they knew who Roy Clarke was.

Today, 41 years after that Villa Park game, Roy Clarke still has slightly mixed feelings. He had scored the winning goal, but had then been carried off and immediately suspected he may be out of action for a while. So upset was he that he cried in the bath afterwards. A few days after the game a newspaper photographer had presented Clarke with a huge enlargement of the photograph of the goal 'with no crowd reaction'. At least he would always have that memory. Not so. It had been in Clarke's possession for just over a week when it was stolen. City had nine league games left before the final, and Clarke's injury would keep him out of the next five. He was back in the side on 16 April in a 1–1 draw at Charlton, and played in front of 50,705 in the 3–1 home victory over Wolves four days later.

The penultimate game of the season saw City lose 6–1 at home to Blackpool with only Paddy Fagan's goal providing any consolation. Clarke's injury had prevented him from playing again, and he was left therefore with just one game to regain full fitness and take his place against Newcastle United at Wembley. The final league game of that 1954–55 season was, ironically, against Aston Villa at Villa Park. City lost the game 2–0, and further tragedy was to strike for Roy Clarke.

'The same thing happened to my knee,' recalls Clarke. 'The Aston Villa full-back came across it again; the same movement, in exactly the same place, and I got carried off again. They put me in the bath and I cried my eyes out. Villa's trainer came in, took my hand and patted me on the back. He said, "Never mind son, you'll be there next year."

That actually happened, almost like Sam Cowan's conversation with the King 32 years earlier.'

Despite his injury, Clarke was determined to support his teammates at Wembley. He remembers travelling down to London with Johnny Hart, a player who had played in all the previous rounds, but whose place in the semi-final had been taken by Bobby Johnstone. Hart too was injured, the victim of a broken leg sustained at Huddersfield just a week before the semi-final.

In those pre-substitute days, the only people allowed to travel on the team bus were the 11 players, the trainer and one reserve. The reserve knew full well that unless a bizarre accident occurred minutes before kick-off, there would be no way he would play. As Clarke says, 'He only went to help put the kit out.'

Because of these separate travelling arrangements, Clarke recalls a humorous incident outside Wembley; 'Johnny Hart and myself couldn't get in. We'd got down too early, and the stewards didn't believe who we were. We had to wait for the coach to come – they all had passes – and we sidled in with them.' As Clarke was reminiscing about the conditions at Villa Park, his mind was taken back to a similar situation in the 1956 FA Cup campaign. On 28 January that year, City were drawn away in the fourth round to Southend United. So waterlogged was the pitch at Roots Hall that day that City were nicknamed 'The Cockleshell Heroes' after the famous Second World War commando raid carried out in small boats. Clarke remembers missing a goal from two yards out when 'a sea-like wave washed the ball behind me just as I was about to tap it into an empty net.' His miss that day did not prove too costly however as Joe Hayes provided the winning goal that would move City further along the road to Wembley and 'Trautmann's Match'.

In the mid 1950s City had some great players in the side and Clarke speaks highly of two in particular – Jack Dyson and Joe Hayes. 'Jack was a good friend of mine, and it was good to see him coming up through the reserves. He was always full of energy, a really natural ball player, and I thought he was as good as, if not better than, that other great footballer-cricketer of the era, Denis Compton.'

High praise for a youngster who not only appeared as an all-rounder for Lancashire during the summer months but would also establish himself in the senior City side in 1955. Dyson's name would appear on the scoresheet for the Blues in the FA Cup final the following year.

Clarke continues: 'Joe Hayes was a young lad from Kearsley near "Bowton" and used to have Johnny Hart as his interpreter. Joe could score goals where nobody else in this world could score goals. If he had 40 players around him and he was facing the other way, if he couldn't move either his leg or his foot, somehow the ball would still end up in the back of the net.

'Joe was a prolific goalscorer [152 in 363 first team appearances], and scored the opening goal in the 1956 FA Cup final. That goal epitomises the whole structure of The Revie Plan. It sums it all up in one movement. From Bill Leivers the full-back to Don Revie who's come deep; he picks up the ball and runs with it before playing it out to myself. Don carries on running, shouting for it back, and Joe Hayes is coming as the front man. I play it diagonally to Don Revie, who then helps it on through the legs of the Birmingham full-back. Joe Hayes comes across and knocks it in. If anyone wants to use the Revie Plan or that kind of system then just look at that goal. It is a marvellous example.'

The Revie Plan was a revolution in British football during the 1950s. I asked Clarke if this plan was worked on in training with blackboards and the like. 'No, we just talked about it,' he replied casually. 'Players in those days expressed themselves a lot more than they do today. Everybody knew instinctively where everybody else would be, and exactly what was expected.' He also goes on to dispel stories that Revie had copied the theory from the great 1953 Hungarian side.

'We played it at Cardiff before the war,' says Clarke. 'I think the first team really to try it seriously was Wolves, captained by Stan Cullis, although they lost the 1939 FA Cup final to Portsmouth. After that game, everyone sort of forgot about the theory.' Early efforts at Maine Road saw reserve team centre-forward Johnny Williamson playing in the deep-lying position later made famous by Don Revie.

As with most professional sportsmen and women, Roy Clarke has recollections of pre-match superstitions: 'I always put my shorts on last. Not for any comfort reasons, simply because I was once told by the trainer that by doing this I would still have a sharp crease in them when I went out onto the pitch. Even if I couldn't play, at least I looked like I could.' Emphasis was also placed on the comfort of his left boot – 'The only one I could use', as opposed to the right – 'It was just for standing on.' In an attempt to boost pride and confidence on derby days, Clarke remembers the whole side would receive a brand new strip just minutes before kick-off.

At the time of his greatest game, Roy Clarke was living in a house in Fallowfield. 'I got married on 1 June 1947, just days after signing for City. We moved up from South Wales and into a house on Victoria Road. The house was just a short walk from the ground, although sometimes I would either chase or catch the bus.'

He had signed for City on 23 May 1947, two months after the transfer deadline, although he still managed to play in the last league game of the 1946–47 season. This game was against his home town team of Newport, on 14 June, a game the Blues won 5–1, with all City's goals coming from inside-left George Smith. Although not 100 per cent certain, Clarke thinks he was allowed to play in the game purely because of the respective positions of both clubs. City had already won the Second Division championship, and Newport had been relegated, therefore whatever the result, it would have no real bearing on either side. The season ran into June purely because of a particularly bad winter, making it the longest ever league season.

As a 21 year-old, Clarke has fond memories of his initial first team meeting, although he remembers being nervous. 'City were playing West Ham and needed the two points to stay top of Division Two. I'd signed on the Friday morning. At the team meeting that morning were Sam Barkas, Frank Swift, Bert Sproston, Joe Fagan, Billy Walsh, Albert Emptage, Andy Black and Eric Westwood – all star players, internationals. I was invited to come to the technical talk on tomorrow's game. I thought, I'm going to learn some words of wisdom here.

'In walked manager Sam Cowan. He sat on a ball on the bench, so he's that bit higher than everyone else. He said, "Well lads, West Ham tomorrow. Get f*****g stuck in and murder them", and walked out of the changing-room. End of team-talk.' So much for words of wisdom!

On 19 September 1958, after 369 league and cup games with 79 goals, 22 Welsh caps and a £1,000 benefit cheque, Roy Clarke left Maine Road and moved to nearby Stockport County. He didn't play many times for the Edgeley Park side, due mainly to a damaged kidney which would bleed on occasion. When his playing days finally came to an end, Clarke became acting manager for a short while before turning to coaching duties, with former Portsmouth player Reg Flewin taking over as manager. After leaving Stockport he moved to non-league Northwich Victoria, once again as acting manager.

By this time he had built up a successful sports goods business in Manchester, and this, coupled with travelling to and from Northwich every day, meant he only stayed in the position for a few months. In 1960 City asked Clarke to return to Maine Road and take over the club's development association office. With the help of two old age pensioners (his words, not mine!), Clarke began to make in the region of £80,000 to £100,000 per year – a great deal of money in the days long before television and sponsorship. 'We ran it from a little brick office at the Platt Lane end. Conditions were not great.'

He continued this work until the end of the 1965–66 season, the year City won the Second Division championship. Then, right out of the blue, he and his wife Kath were asked to manage the Manchester City social club. To this day he has no idea why: 'Why they gave me the job, I don't know. I had no catering and licensing experience, and was teetotal!'

The new job immediately took over his life, so much so that, by his own admission, he neglected his sports businesses (he now had three shops), and was forced to sell them. 'I was so interested in the new job. For me entertainment and football are the same thing. We had some wonderful acts at the club – Frankie Vaughan, Ken Dodd, Mike Yarwood, Vince Hill and Bob Monkhouse all performed there and, of course, we had the players' Christmas pantomimes.' Even today, though, Roy Clarke turns pale at the thought of Lovelace Watkins' one-night appearance fee: '£300 we paid him – mind you he did start out asking for more.'

In 1996, unbelievably nearly 50 years after arriving at Maine Road for the first time, Roy Clarke is still connected with Manchester City Football Club. He is currently secretary of the club's former players' association, an organisation which has in the region of 150 members. They have regular get-togethers and generally take care of former players who have fallen on difficult times.

Even on first team match days, 'Nobby' can be found at Maine Road. He told me, 'I've got a job. I don't get paid, though! I look after the sponsors. I take them on a tour of the ground and tell them some stories – including a few lies.'

I can think of no one better-qualified to do this job than Roy Clarke. He is without doubt a marvellous ambassador for Manchester City Football Club, and I felt proud and privileged to have spent an afternoon (although I'm sure it could easily have gone on longer) in his company. Long may his connection with the club continue.

Saturday, 26 March 1955

FA Cup semi-final at Villa Park

Manchester City	1	(Clarke)
Sunderland	0	

MANCHESTER CITY	v.	SUNDERLAND
Bert Trautmann	1	Willie Fraser
Jimmy Meadows	2	Jack Hedley
Roy Little	3	Joe McDonald
Ken Barnes	4	Stan Anderson
Dave Ewing	5	Ray Daniel
Roy Paul	6	George Aitken
Paddy Fagan	7	Billy Bingham
Joe Hayes	8	Charlie Fleming
Don Revie	9	Ted Purdon
Bobby Johnstone	10	Len Shackleton
Roy Clarke	11	Billy Elliott

Attendance: 58,498

Manager

TONY BOOK

City v. Newcastle United
Football League Cup final at Wembley Stadium, 28 February 1976

When a 30 year-old part-time footballer arrived at Maine Road in the World-Cup-winning summer of 1966, no one could have foreseen the influence he would have on Manchester City Football Club. Tony Book was that man who, before his retirement seven years later, would become City's most successful captain of all time. It would be Book's hands which lifted the First Division championship trophy, the FA Cup, the European Cup Winners' Cup and the Football League Cup all in the space of a glorious three seasons.

In April 1974 Book became manager and began a successful spell arguably second only to the legendary partnership of Joe Mercer and Malcolm Allison. Over the next five years City finished eighth, eighth, second, fourth and 15th in Division One. They played three consecutive seasons in the UEFA Cup and reached the fifth round of the League Cup twice as well as winning that same trophy in 1976.

I caught up with Tony Book earlier this year at the ground and we talked about that League Cup triumph of 20 years ago – the manager's choice of Blue Heaven.

In 1970 goals by Mike Doyle and Glyn Pardoe had won the League Cup final against West Bromwich Albion. Six years on it was Peter Barnes and Dennis Tueart who were City's Wembley winners against

Gordon Lee's Newcastle United side. Book was captain in 1970 and manager in 1976, becoming the first man ever to win the League Cup in both these positions. 'Three days before the final we took the side down to a health centre near Tring,' recalls Book, 'and I remember we were billeted in small chalets just outside the main building. Dave Watson had a problem with his back at the time. I used to do my rounds and check the players were all right, and every time I went into Dave's room I'd find him lying on the floor. He was very doubtful for the game and in the end he did really well to play.

'The only other problem I had was who to play at right-back. Kenny Clements and Colin Barrett had played in earlier rounds but were both out injured and so in the end I picked young Ged Keegan. He'd only played there once before but did a good job for me.'

Two other incidents are still strong in Tony Book's mind. 'The first one is Peter Barnes's goal. This was a move we'd practised a lot in training: a cross to the far post, a header back in and then the finish. That goal gave me a lot of pleasure.'

The second was the injury to Colin Bell. 'Colin had been seriously injured in the fourth round win over United. He was almost impossible to replace. I tried really hard for one particular replacement, going in very strongly to the board to try and sign Alan Ball from Arsenal.

'I knew Colin was going to be out for a long time because the medical staff had told me. Alan's dad had contacted me and told me Alan was available. Anyway the board had a vote and my request was turned down. I was disappointed because I knew what a good player Alan was. He was the right type to come in at that particular moment and I knew he would fit into the team well. We had a useful side and I felt sure we would have gone on and won trophies. He was a born leader and would have been an asset to the team.'

What was the relationship like between Tony and his assistant manager Ian McFarlane? 'I'd known Ian as a player at Bath City but since then he'd been at Sheffield Wednesday and later Middlesbrough with Jack Charlton. When I took over I knew what was needed and I knew that we'd work well together. It was a bit like Joe and Malcolm, I suppose. Ian was the loud, hard man. The lads certainly enjoyed him. He worked well with the players and was very strong in his views.

'It was a difficult time when he left us. It all came about because he still had this property up in the north-east. He asked the club if they would buy it off him because he'd already taken out a mortgage on a property down here. When the club said they wouldn't, Ian thought it was time to move on and he left straight after the final. It was a great shame because we had a good partnership and the team was playing so well.'

Whilst Book was searching for a replacement, he contacted the Leeds United manager and former City player Don Revie. Revie suggested Book should perhaps consider the quietly spoken Fulham and England coach Bill Taylor. This he did, and Taylor arrived at Maine Road to continue the good work started by McFarlane – albeit not quite as loudly.

Having checked the record books, Book's reign as manager did not see a great deal of players leaving Maine Road. This is always the sign of a happy, successful side. Perhaps the most famous player to be transferred during this period was Rodney Marsh.

'That was a difficult decision to make,' comments Book. 'He was always the fans' favourite but I could never get him playing consistently well for the club at the time. To win trophies you have to have consistency in your players. Like I say, it was a difficult decision but it was one I felt I had to make.'

Among Book's signings were Brian Kidd, Joe Royle, Dave Watson and Asa Hartford. Showing not even a hint of arrogance, Tony Book is justifiably proud of these signings: 'They were all good signings. We got Asa after Leeds United turned him down because of a supposed hole in the heart. I remember Ken Barnes saying at the time, "If he's got a hole in the heart, then there's something wrong with all of us." Ken was the scout at the time so I took his advice and brought him in.

'Dave Watson came in on the recommendation of Ian McFarlane who'd worked with him at Sunderland. When Dave came in I moved Tommy Booth into midfield. Tommy perhaps struggled a little for pace but he had always been a skilful player. I had no hesitation in playing him at number eight in the final.'

City's quest for the 1976 Football League Cup began at Norwich in September the previous year. Dave Watson's goal was enough to earn a draw and bring the Canaries back to Maine Road for a replay the following week. Another close game ensued and although City scored twice thanks to Dennis Tueart and Joe Royle, the game finished 2–2. The tie would have to be decided on a neutral ground and Chelsea's Stamford Bridge was chosen.

A crowd of just over 6,000 witnessed a terrific Blues performance, and Norwich were crushed 6–1. After two very evenly balanced games what was the difference? Tony Book recalls: 'Rodney Marsh, pure and simple. We all knew what a great talent he had, but that night he was outstanding. That game at Stamford Bridge was one of the best games I'd ever seen him have. He was full of himself and cheeky – the way he played the game. Everything he tried came off. It just proved to everyone what we already knew – he really was an outstanding talent. He put on a great show.'

Perhaps Marsh's biggest disappointment that night was the fact that he missed out on scoring. Dennis Tueart didn't, though, – scoring three, with Joe Royle, Mike Doyle and an own goal providing the others.

Injury to Tueart meant a return to the first team for Peter Barnes for the visit of Nottingham Forest in the next round. City's team contained nine full internationals and it was two of their England men – Joe Royle (his third goal in three games) and Colin Bell – who provided the goals in a 2–1 win. Forest's goal was scored by former City player Ian Bowyer.

The fourth round brought Manchester United and a crowd of 50,000 to Maine Road for a match described earlier in this book, chosen as Asa Hartford's idea of Blue Heaven. The game on 12 November was as one-sided as any derby game has ever been, Dennis Tueart opening the scoring for the Blues after just 35 seconds. Asa Hartford extended the lead before Tueart scored his sixth League Cup goal of the season and the Blues went in at half-time with a 3–0 lead.

Joe Royle made it 4–0 (and four goals in four games for himself), but the game was marred by the horrendous injury to Colin Bell. Book recalls, 'The injuries to Colin Bell and Glyn Pardoe cost Manchester City an awful lot. I feel sure both could have gone on and played into their late 30s. They were strong, fit boys and I'm certain the club wouldn't have had the troubles we've had if it hadn't been for those injuries. They both worked tremendously hard to get back, as did Paul Lake more recently. They all went through hell but unfortunately it didn't happen for any of them.'

Third Division Mansfield Town provided the opposition in round five. Tommy Booth replaced the injured Colin Bell in midfield as the Blues ran out 4–2 winners. The goals that night were scored by Asa Hartford, Alan Oakes and the two 'old dependables' – Joe Royle (five in five) and Dennis Tueart (seven in four).

Royle and Tueart's marvellous goalscoring runs ended at the usually scarce (even nowadays) picking ground of Middlesbrough in the first leg of the semi-final. The Blues lost 1–0 in the game played on 13 January.

'We played some marvellous football in the return leg,' remembers Book today. 'It was a cracking game. Injuries meant I had to play several youngsters but on the night they all did me proud and we ran out 4–0 winners.' Ged Keegan levelled the tie on aggregate before goals from Alan Oakes, Peter Barnes and Joe Royle confirmed City's trip to Wembley.

The final took place on 28 February 1976. It is a date etched on all Blues' followers' minds, because it is the last day City won a major competition. Preparations by both sides for the game could not have been different. City spent a leisurely few days at a health centre near Tring, and apart from the problem with Dave Watson's back forcing him to spend two nights sleeping on the bedroom floor, the only other minor irritation was the food.

'As with all these health centres, the place we stayed at was very diet conscious. One of the things the lads liked during the build-up to games – especially on the Thursdays and Fridays – was chips. They were very disappointed when they couldn't get any!'

Newcastle, on the other hand, had many more serious problems. Because of a flu epidemic sweeping the north-east, they had only six fit men just 24 hours prior to kick-off. If you look closely at the team photograph on the match-day programme, this could perhaps offer an explanation. The ground is covered with snow and to a man, every single one of them looks frozen stiff.

Goalkeeper Mike Mahoney was suffering more than most and had to spend four days confined to bed. Manager Gordon Lee commented, 'No team has ever had a worse build-up to a Cup final.'

Tony Book remembers the League Cup final of two years before. 'That really was just one of those days. We had a magnificent attack but on the day their keeper stopped everything. He had a marvellous game.'

Would the memories of that Wolves game have any bearing against Newcastle? 'Because of the way we'd played in the earlier rounds I was confident of victory. If you look at the teams we'd played – Norwich City, Nottingham Forest and United, and especially the way we played against Middlesbrough in the semi-final – they were all good sides. We'd scored lots of goals and the defence had been tight throughout.' (City had scored 23 and conceded eight in the eight games leading up to the final.) 'The team was full of themselves – they knew they were capable of going out and winning it.'

What about the youngsters? 'I've always had an opinion about young players: if they're good enough, they go in. As long as you've got seven or eight experienced players around them you should put them in. Ged Keegan, for instance, was really thrown in at the deep end. It was only his second game at right-back but he gave a sound performance on the day. I was delighted for him. Although Paul Power didn't play in the final he had such a good engine and had no difficulties in getting up and down the pitch. Peter Barnes had all the ability in the world. I was never frightened in taking a chance with any of them.'

And so to Wembley, where the 100,000 capacity crowd witnessed the unusual sight of assistant manager and coach Ian McFarlane – sporting a very natty checked cap – walking out with the side. The match was to be refereed by Jack Taylor, the man who had taken charge of the 1974 World Cup final. Taylor was highly respected and thought by many to be the best referee in the world.

If the Geordies were suffering any ill effects, they certainly didn't show it. They laid early siege to the Blues' goal with Joe Corrigan being called upon to make two clearances in the opening 90 seconds.

Peter Barnes's first touch of the game produced a shot by Asa Hartford which struck team-mate Dennis Tueart before being cleared by the Magpies' defence. Corrigan was called into action again when a shot by Malcolm Macdonald was turned behind for a corner. Keegan blocked another Macdonald effort as the Blues struggled to find any kind of rhythm. Corrigan cleared the lines with a long kick aimed towards Joe Royle. Newcastle's centre-half Glenn Keeley went up with Royle and was penalised – somewhat harshly – for a push in the back on the Blues' striker.

Keegan and Hartford both placed the ball for the free-kick, and it

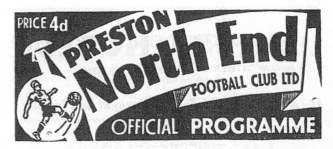

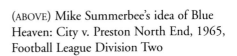

(ABOVE) Mike Summerbee's idea of Blue Heaven: City v. Preston North End, 1965, Football League Division Two

(LEFT) Still smiling after all these years . . . Mike Summerbee, one of the game's great characters

(ABOVE) Injury prevented Colin Bell from playing for City and England for two years. In his first game back the Blues beat Newcastle United 4–0 (© Manchester City FC)

(LEFT) Pictured outside the Platt Lane complex, Colin looks as fit today as he did when he was playing

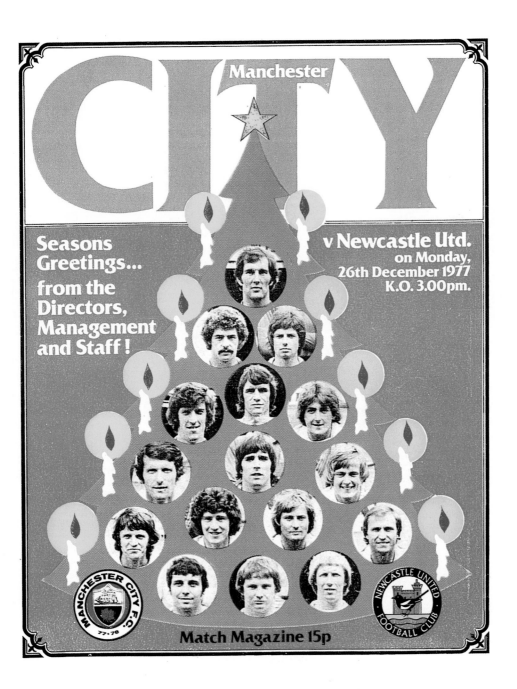

(ABOVE) Colin's Blue Heaven was the match against Newcastle United in 1977

BARCLAYS LEAGUE DIVISION ONE

MANCHESTER CITY

versus
DERBY COUNTY
SATURDAY, 20th APRIL, 1991.
KICK-OFF: 3.00 p.m.

OFFICIAL MATCH MAGAZINE £1.00

(ABOVE) Blue Heaven for Niall Quinn was against Derby County at Maine Road in 1991

(RIGHT) Niall Quinn in his usual colours during the 1995–96 season . . .

(BELOW) . . . and leaving the pitch after his heroics as stand-in goalkeeper against Derby County (both © Manchester City FC)

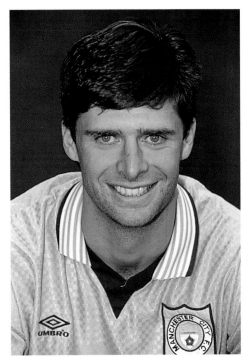

(RIGHT) Asa Hartford's Blue
Heaven: City v. United in the
League Cup in 1975

(BELOW) Asa, the current
assistant manager. 'If he's
got a hole in the heart, then
there's something wrong
with all of us.'

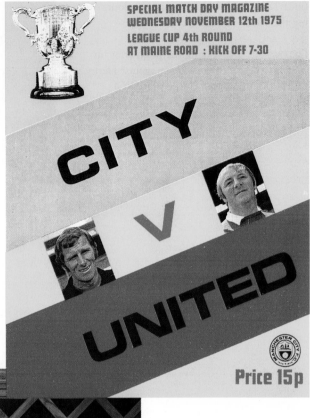

SPECIAL MATCH DAY MAGAZINE
WEDNESDAY NOVEMBER 12th 1975
LEAGUE CUP 4th ROUND
AT MAINE ROAD : KICK OFF 7-30

CITY
v
UNITED

Price 15p

OPPOSITE
(TOP AND FAR RIGHT) Blue
Heaven for Roy Clarke: City
v. Sunderland in the 1955 FA
Cup semi-final

(RIGHT) Roy pictured in his
beloved Social Club at Maine
Road in 1996. Roy assured
me that he hadn't been
fighting!

OFFICIAL PROGRAMME

THE FOOTBALL ASSOCIATION
CHALLENGE CUP

SEMI-FINAL TIE

Photograph by A. Wilkes & Son, West Bromwich.

MANCHESTER CITY
v.
SUNDERLAND

LA PARK. BIRMINGHAM

URDAY, MARCH 26th 1955

KICK-OFF 2-30 p.m.

PRICE **6** D. ISSUED BY
ASTON VILLA F.C.

(LEFT AND BELOW) Tony Book's idea of Blue Heaven was against Newcastle United at Wembley in the 1976 League Cup final

MANCHESTER CITY

SATURDAY, 28th FEBRUARY 1976 · Kick-off 3.3

THE FOOTBALL LEAGUE

CUP FINAL

WEMBLEY STADIUM

Official Souvenir Programme . . . . Twenty pence

THE EMPIRE STADIUM, WEMBLEY

THE
**FOOTBALL
LEAGUE
CUP
FINAL**
SAT., FEB. 28, 1976

KICK-OFF 3.30 p.m.
YOU ARE ADVISED TO TAKE UP
YOUR POSITION BY 3 p.m.

TURNSTILES
D
ENTRANCE
9

591

**EAST
STANDING
ENCLOSURE**

CHAIRMAN:
WEMBLEY STADIUM LTD

STANDING
£1.50
TO BE RETAINED   SEE PLAN AND CONDITIONS ON BACK

NEWCASTLE UNITED

(RIGHT) Pictured at Maine Road, Tony Book recalls memories of 30 years with Manchester City FC

was Hartford's cross to the far post which City captain Mike Doyle headed back across the goal. A crowd of players including Royle, Keeley and Newcastle's former Blackpool star Mickey Burns all went up for it, but the ball fell invitingly for Peter Barnes who smashed it home with his favoured left foot from the six-yard line. Only 12 minutes had been played and already there had been goalmouth incidents at both ends and City were a goal to the good.

Tommy Booth and Alan Oakes both had shots wide of the target and Corrigan made a brave, diving save at the feet of the on-rushing (but, as it happened, offside) Macdonald.

Newcastle levelled the score with ten minutes to go before half-time when Hartford lost possession to Alan Kennedy on City's right wing. The ball was worked across the pitch to the ever-dangerous Macdonald, whose low cross was turned past Corrigan by the outstretched leg of Alan Gowling for his 24th goal of the season.

Tueart should have restored City's lead when Donachie's long free-kick found him completely unmarked on the edge of the six-yard box. Somehow Mahoney managed to block the shot with his legs and the ball ran out for a corner. Corrigan foiled Newcastle's next attack with another brave block at Macdonald's feet before Oakes spread the play wide to Donachie out on the left. His first time cross was met by Tueart, who unfortunately could not get over the ball and agonisingly headed over.

It was the last incident of the first half. The teams went in level at 1–1 – a fair indication of the first 45 minutes' play. The first two minutes of the second half provided two more scoring opportunities for Dennis Tueart, the man picked out before the game by Newcastle as City's danger-man. The first one saw his cross-shot go wide of a gaping Newcastle goal. The second was the stuff dreams are made of. It turned out to be the winning goal as well as being arguably the most spectacular ever scored at Wembley.

Willie Donachie moved forward in what used to be known as the inside-left position. His cross was headed back by Tommy Booth towards Tueart, who had his back to goal on the penalty spot. Tueart's tremendous athleticism and volleying ability provided a memorable overhead kick and the ball flew past a diving Mahoney. It was Tueart's 20th goal of the season. Photographs of that spectacular moment adorned thousands of walls for many months to come.

City's lead appeared to have been increased when Joe Royle chipped the goalkeeper from 25 yards, only to have his effort disallowed for offside. Booth saw his header go wide, whilst at the other end Burns shot across goal and then forced Corrigan to make another fine save from a header. First aid was applied to a cut above Watson's eye shortly before the Geordies wasted another chance after Doyle was penalised for handball just outside the penalty area.

There was certainly no shortage of incidents. With just five minutes to go, a left-foot shot from Gowling was goal-bound before being tipped over by the ever-alert Joe Corrigan. Seconds later Mahoney was the hero as he saved Booth's header from a Tueart corner. Booth's header turned out to be the last chance of the game. Jack Taylor blew the final whistle and Mike Doyle – man of the match, according to Tueart – punched the ground in jubilation. The match-winner then exchanged shirts with Newcastle's number three, Alan Kennedy.

Doyle led the victorious side up the famous Wembley steps to receive the Football League Cup from the Duke of Norfolk. On their way down the whole side was greeted with tremendously sporting applause and congratulations from the obviously bitterly disappointed Geordie fans. Twice in three seasons they had suffered a Wembley defeat, having lost 3–0 to Liverpool in the 1974 FA Cup final.

City's 'number one' fan 'Big Helen' Turner joined the Blues on their lap of honour. Later, in the changing-rooms, Dave Watson had a single stitch put in his eye wound and Dennis Tueart took both the Cup and the champagne in to the losers. Newcastle skipper Tommy Craig was gracious in defeat, in no way putting the result down to the flu epidemic and saying, 'On the day, City deserved to win.'

The Grosvenor Hotel staged the victory banquet later that evening. After the meal Book remembers, 'We had a cabaret; I think it was Roy Clarke who'd organised it. The singer was a young blond lad – I can't remember his name – and for some reason I came away with his trilby.' Thank goodness Tom Jones wasn't on!

In nearly ten years City, under Book as either captain or manager, had averaged a trophy every other season.

Apart from brother Kim – forever remembered as the unfortunate Northampton goalkeeper who conceded eight (George Best six) goals to Manchester United in an FA Cup tie – did Tony have any other family football connections? 'No, I came from an army background, really. My father enlisted in the army as a young lad and joined the Somerset Light Infantry. He started off as a bugle boy and ended up doing 30 years' service. We went abroad and I lived in India for seven years. I used to play out there – in bare feet – and I suppose it was really where I learned to play.

'I came back when I was 11 and started to play at school, and it went on from there. I've got six brothers, two of whom also spent long periods in the army, and we could all do a bit. The one brother that's older than me – Mervyn – he had a lot more ability than me and could, and should, have made it. But he didn't like the training. He wouldn't work at it and so he fell by the wayside. I suppose I was the lucky one.'

From school Book progressed to Bath Boys and later Somerset Boys. 'There were lots of rumours about me: I was going to go here, I was going to go there. Bristol Rovers were said to be interested in me, as were Nottingham Forest. I remember that Forest arranged a charity game and asked me to play in a mixed side against them. It was meant to be my trial game. Albert Quixall played for us and Joe Mercer, manager of Aston Villa at the time, took charge of us. I was playing for Bath City then and the club was told to send someone else with me – for company, I suppose. The lad that came with me was a centre-forward called Colin Merson. Forest were supposed to be looking at me, but in the end they turned me down and signed Colin on. That's how things work out sometimes in football.'

As with other members of his family, Tony too has spent time in the army. 'I was serving with the Royal Army Medical Corps when I got the opportunity to play in the reserves at Chelsea. I was doing all right when one day I got this letter from manager Ted Drake saying I'd done well but he didn't think I was up to First Division standard. He went on to say why not lower my sights and try again somewhere else.'

Following his National Service that's exactly what Book did do. He continues, 'I went to play for a Western League team call Peasedown Miners. Peasedown is a small village just outside Bath where my wife comes from. I then signed on a part-time professional basis for Frome Town, who were a first division side in the Western League.

'We got knocked out of the Cup in the very early stages and I got a letter through the door at home. It said the club wanted to cut my wages from £5 per week to £2 10s per week! I was working for a building firm at the time run by Arthur Mortimore, the chairman of Bath City. On one particular day I showed the letter to one of the company's clerks who happened to be on the site. He asked me if he could hang on to it, and a few days later Bath made an offer for me. Frome accepted the offer and I stayed at Bath for 11 seasons.'

It was at Bath that Book met Malcolm Allison for the first time. Little did either know then what a phenomenal working relationship would develop over the next few years.

'When Malcolm came, things really began to happen. Like most non-league clubs we used to train on Tuesdays and Thursdays. When he arrived – all bright and breezy – we used to train three nights a week and on Sundays before the season started. We won the Southern League championship when he was there and I think he just saw something in me. Then one day he got a job offer in Canada with Toronto City. Not long afterwards he phoned me and said he'd got a job for me out there. It came as a real shock. I was about 29 and I'd never flown before. I went to Heathrow for a flight to New York. I didn't know what the hell I was doing – I couldn't even put the bloody seat-belt on! When I got to New York I thought, "Christ, what's all this about?" Remember, I was just a simple country boy.

'I had a great time in Canada, playing against some good Italian sides, and then Malcolm gets the job at Plymouth. I was in Canada for just the summer, but still under contract to Bath. Malcolm bid £2,500 for me when he got back and at first Bath didn't want to let me go. I said, "Come on, give me a chance. I've been here for 11 seasons, and this might be my last opportunity." I played two seasons for Plymouth without missing a game, before coming to City in 1966. Apart from six months with Cardiff in 1980–81, I've been here ever since.'

On 30 November 1973 Tony Book finally retired from playing at the grand old age of 38. He became assistant manager to Ron Saunders, and when Saunders left Maine Road five months later, the club had no hesitation in offering the manager's job to the ever-dependable defender from the West Country. A highly successful five years for Manchester City had begun.

Malcolm Allison returned to Maine Road for a second spell as manager in July 1979. Or did he? Tony Book tells a different story.

'No, I was still manager. Malcolm was brought back as my assistant and coach but I knew there was no chance of that working. Bill Taylor had left and the club wanted Malcolm back, but I wasn't for it at all.

'My relationship with Malcolm was strictly player-to-manager. Although I'd obviously known him for a number of years, you couldn't really describe the relationship as a friendship. It was purely a working relationship – I played and he managed. From day one it was never going to work – Malcolm just took over.'

In October the following year the partnership was over. In Tony Book's own words, 'We both got the sack. It was then that I moved to Cardiff. It didn't seem anything like six months; the time went so quickly it was almost like I had never been away.' Fortunately, Book had the presence of mind to keep his house in Sale – one of three he has had in the area since his move to Manchester 30 years ago – and would fly to and from Cardiff on a regular basis.

He continues the story: 'Then one day, right out of the blue, I got a call from John Bond. He asked me to come back and look after the youth development side. I had worked alongside Ken Barnes, who was chief scout, for about two months when John said he didn't want me working in the office any longer. He said he wanted me to come out and work with the kids. That's how it all started again. We won the Youth Cup and then I took the reserves for a spell and eventually moved into my present position as first team coach.

'I enjoy what I do now. Alan Ball's been great with me – he just lets me get on with it. Providing I don't let him down, he's told me that as long as he's around, he wants me to stay. How long it will go on for I just don't know. I'd love to do another couple of years. One of the reasons I've lasted so long and want to stay on is that I want to see the club successful again. That's my aim. I'd love to be here when they win another trophy. I could then go away knowing that the club was back on the right road.

'The fans here deserve something and have been terrific over the years. They are the real reason I came back. Being an ex-captain I was invited to Wembley for the Centenary FA Cup final of 1981. When I was introduced to the crowd I got a fantastic reception from the City fans. I hadn't made my mind up then whether or not to come back. They made it up for me.'

The club's most successful captain and without doubt one of their most successful and popular managers has one final memory of that 1976 Football League Cup final: 'I remember the coat I wore – brown with really wide lapels. It was a good coat, that, and I've still got it in the wardrobe at home!'

Saturday, 28 February 1976

Football League Cup final at Wembley Stadium

Manchester City	2	(Barnes, Tueart)
Newcastle United	1	(Gowling)

MANCHESTER CITY	v.	NEWCASTLE UNITED
Joe Corrigan	1	Mike Mahoney
Ged Keegan	2	Irving Nattrass
Willie Donachie	3	Alan Kennedy
Mike Doyle	4	Stewart Barrowclough
Dave Watson	5	Glenn Keeley
Alan Oakes	6	Pat Howard
Peter Barnes	7	Micky Burns
Tommy Booth	8	Tommy Cassidy
Joe Royle	9	Malcolm Macdonald
Asa Hartford	10	Alan Gowling
Dennis Tueart	11	Tommy Craig
Kenny Clements	SUB	Paul Cannell

Attendance: 100,000

ON THE BENCH

By now you've probably read – and hopefully enjoyed – the memories of the players. Over the next few pages you will find the recollections of other 'True Blues', by their own admissions not quite good enough to make the first team, but nevertheless famous in their own fields.

JAMES H. REEVE

JAMES H. REEVE, broadcaster, cricketer, available 24 hours a day –
'No job too small.'

'Funnily enough I was asked this same question earlier this year at
a branch meeting of the Prestwich Supporters' Club. In all honesty, as
age creeps up on you, the euphoria of youth tends to diminish slightly.
Having said that, though, I will always remember the famous 4–3
victory at Newcastle as well as the 3–1 win at Old Trafford just a few
weeks earlier.

'I also remember a cup replay against Blackpool – I think they had
Alan Ball playing – played on a Wednesday night in front of a crowd
of nearly 53,000. But perhaps the most impressive game I remember
– I'd be about 16 – was at Maine Road in February 1966, an FA Cup
tie against Leicester City. In those days we always seemed to play
Leicester in a cup competition.

'It was raining heavily and although we were at home, I remember
City played in their all-maroon change kit. After about 20 minutes we
were 2–0 down. City eventually levelled the score thanks to two goals
from Neil Young and later won the replay at Filbert Street. I have to
say that I have never seen or heard a Maine Road crowd more
influential on the team's performance than that night. Everybody in
the ground seemed to be willing the ball in for a third goal.

'When I got back home highlights of the game were shown on
television. These were the days of cameras perched on a gantry under
the Kippax roof, and an army of sky-blue invalid carriages surrounded

171

the pitch. As is often the case, the television cameras see things that spectators miss at games and I will never forget one particular incident.

'In an attempt to get that third goal City were attacking down the left wing. The play moved past this chap who was watching the game from the relative comfort of his bath chair. It was one of those big basket things with three wheels and a huge tiller. He was so beside himself that in his excitement he flung himself out of his chair! Quite simply he had gone berserk, and that vision of a flying quilt and old-fashioned NHS crutches has stayed with me ever since.'

NICK CONWAY

NICK CONWAY, actor, toured the country with Tom Watt in *An Evening with Gary Lineker*, instantly recognisable to millions as Billy Boswell in the top-rated television comedy series *Bread*.

'My first memories of watching City were when I was about eight or nine. I think it was in the 1970–71 season – the season before Francis Lee scored all those penalties – and I went with my dad to a midweek game against Blackpool. We couldn't get seats and so we had to stand on the Kippax. We stood right at the back on some metal girder-like things and I remember almost bending double trying to see the pitch under the roof. From that night I was hooked; the atmosphere was fantastic.

'From the 1972–73 season I began to go regularly. We used to sit in the old Platt Lane Stand and everybody seemed to me to be a grandad! There were flat caps, tartan rugs and flasks everywhere! In one particular game I remember an old man losing his false teeth in the excitement. They fell out and went under one of the benches and all the young supporters began crawling about on all fours looking for them!

'I also remember the 3–3 game with United and I have to confess that I was one of the many 'snorkel parkas' sat on the front wall in the Kippax. I'll never forget coming back from Wembley after the 1974 League Cup final. The Wolves fans were all laughing. All I could do was cry.

'Of all the games I've seen though, the one I most remember has to be the 5–1 against United in 1989. The game was played around the same time that *Bread* was really well known and I'd met Mel Machin's wife just a few weeks earlier. Because of this meeting I'd been invited behind the scenes a few times but none of them could compare with the scenes and emotions after the derby.

'Mel Machin had this reputation of being very serious all the time, so much so that people actually called him a "miserable git". But I can tell you that he certainly wasn't miserable that night. He was so proud of all his team you just wouldn't have believed it. I have to say that he was one of the nicest men I've ever met.

'The celebratory scenes around Cheadle and Didsbury that night will stay with me forever. It's funny how life turns out sometimes – I thought before the game we might get stuffed!'

STAN GIBSON

STAN GIBSON, undoubtedly a Maine Road legend; the man who for over 35 years has been responsible for making the Maine Road playing surface one of the finest in the country.

'In my younger days, especially during my time in the navy, I'd always loved sport. Even if I say so myself I wasn't bad at football. I used to be a centre-forward and even managed a few trial games for City's A team. Unfortunately I never made the grade and I eventually became groundsman at Chorlton Cricket Club. In 1960 the City board approached me and offered me the job at Maine Road. Naturally I said yes and I've been here ever since.

'I've seen so many things here including the great Bert Trautmann being sent off. He was in a shocking mood as I walked down the tunnel with him. His language was awful – good job it was in German! I've also seen lots of things I daren't tell you about!

'I had a stroke not so long ago and unfortunately my memory is not as good as it used to be, but two games will always stand out. I have some great recollections of the 1969 FA Cup final against Leicester, but the game I will never forget was the 4–3 win at Newcastle.

'I can still see those goals now, and what made it better was United lost at home to Sunderland so the league was definitely ours. I think it was when the third goal went in that everyone around me threw their hats into the air. I threw mine along with them and never saw it again! I was upset about that – it was my lucky mascot! We stopped

175

off somewhere on the way back for a big party and a slap-up meal. I felt like I was boozed up all day! It really was out of this world. I've never been so happy.

'The Maine Road pitch really is my pride and joy. I love it. I have two lads working with me nowadays – we also look after Platt Lane – but they know how I feel about the pitch and so they don't interfere! I do get a bit depressed when the club stages a pop concert on it, though. I know this is the way of things in the 1990s but with all the weight of the stage and the crowds on it, my pitch drops two inches every time we have one.

'At the moment I can't see myself ever retiring from the job. I think I'll probably die on the pitch. Might not be a bad thing, that. The club have already agreed to have my ashes scattered on it when I've gone!'

GARY JAMES

GARY JAMES, co-author of *The Pride of Manchester*, the complete record of all City–United games, and the bestselling *Football with a Smile: The Authorised Biography of Joe Mercer*.

'I suppose my earliest memories are of being taken to Maine Road by my parents when I was about two or three. They would take me regularly to reserve games at that time and would convince me I was watching the first team. The first game I can remember in any real detail was Rodney Marsh's debut against Chelsea in 1972. I remember Marsh had this thing of not wearing any socks – apart from when he was playing, of course – and for some reason that appealed to me at the time. I suppose he was my first City hero.

'One game more than most others still stands out in my mind. It took place in March 1985, a 1–0 win at Blackburn. City were going for promotion that season and it was the first season that I'd travelled regularly to away games. On all these away games we seemed to take over the ground and outnumber the home fans. This always made for a great atmosphere.

'Steve Kinsey scored the only goal that day, and if memory serves, it took us to the top of the league. This was the Blackburn prior to Jack Walker, and I can recall standing in the Main Stand paddock after a walk along several *Coronation Street* -style streets.

'Everyone was in fine voice on the way back to Manchester on the train after the game. We got off the train at Victoria Station and walked straight into a crowd of Everton fans – they'd just drawn 1–1 at Old Trafford – who were making their way home. It was the first real taste of any crowd trouble I'd ever experienced and I ran as fast as I could towards the old *Daily Mirror* building.

'I remember running up a small side street near *The Daily Mirror* and ran into a policeman who forced me against a wall where I hurt my knee. He then told me to go back the way I came, back towards the station. I turned the corner and to my delight I found myself in a joyous band of Mancunians singing loudly, "We're the pride of Manchester." Safe at last – or so I thought!

'Two minutes later I discovered to my horror that they were United fans! I decided to just play along for a while and it was at this point that I found my separated friend, Paul Alexander. He joined the crowd and we slowly moved along Market Street towards Piccadilly Gardens. Sometime later we managed to escape and finally arrived in the safe surroundings of Piccadilly Station for our train back to Hyde.

'That night my family attended a party at the local cricket club, and because I'd had nothing to eat all day, the beer found no resistance and I was drunk very quickly. It was then that I had to tell my dad about the crowd trouble and my "run-in" with the law.

'I don't know what was worse – telling him what had happened or being spotted in a crowd of United fans!'

JOHN MADDOCKS

JOHN MADDOCKS, former English teacher and now City's official historian and statistician. In true historian style, John remembers the exact date of his most memorable match.

'November 5 1983. Shrewsbury Town 1 City 3. By no means a "big" game, but everything about the day was just perfect. It was a beautiful, crisp, bright November day and we had a trouble-free trip down. I remember getting to our seats in the main stand and we all burst out laughing at the crowd segregation. It was just a clothes line stretched from the top of the stand down to the pitch with not a steward in sight!

'Shortly before kick-off the "ball collector" made his way around the cinder track with his coracle towards the nearby River Severn. City had lost 5–0 the previous week at Newcastle whereas Shrewsbury had lost only one of their last seven games. It looked like a difficult game for the Blues, who had Nicky Reid back from injury.

'Despite Graham Baker's terrific performance in midfield the teams went in goalless at half-time. In the second half things were different. Andy May flicked in Paul Power's corner to give City the lead, Tommy Caton scored with a 25-yarder before Steve Kinsey made it 3–0 with just ten minutes left.

'When they were three down Shrewsbury started to play. Cross pulled one back with five minutes to go and then Alex Williams saw a shot from McNally hit the inside of his left-hand post. City were apparently doing their utmost to "snatch a draw from the jaws of victory".

'I also remember some bangers being thrown onto the pitch when City were two up, and one seemed to hit the referee. He immediately threatened to take both teams off, before a heartfelt plea from Billy McNeill changed his mind. A message was broadcast on the public address system and the game continued.

'After the game a few pints were made very welcome in a riverside pub before we adjourned to an Italian restaurant for a super meal. On the way back home we witnessed several bonfires and fireworks. All in all, it was a memorable day out.'

VINCE MILLER

VINCE MILLER, former radio broadcaster, now a much-in-demand master of ceremonies, perhaps most famous for his pre-match introductions on the Maine Road pitch.

'I've been watching City since 1948, and to be perfectly honest it's very difficult to remember one particular match. During that time, though, there have been many memorable incidents.

'I can remember in the early 1970s I used to cover City's games for Piccadilly Radio. Even then Tom Tyrell reported on United, and I do remember this particular midweek game – against Spurs, I think – at Maine Road. Bill Shankly was at the game as a guest of Bobby Charlton and it was the same day Shanks had resigned from Anfield. I was the first radio reporter to interview him. He was really down in the dumps, and it was a great scoop for the station.

'We would also scour the local newspapers to see which stars were appearing in Manchester either in stage productions or in concert. One Saturday, David Essex was in town at the Free Trade Hall and we invited him to the game in the afternoon. He said he would have to leave about four o'clock in order to get back in time for rehearsals.

'At half-time we went into the players' lounge where David gleefully tucked into a meat and potato pie. He said he had never tasted pies as nice as these before and later telephoned me and asked for a quantity to be sent over to the Free Trade Hall.

'I can also remember the times when things weren't so enjoyable as well. I remember being next to Denis Law in the changing-room at a reserve game shortly after his famous back-heel had relegated United. He had had a nightmare game and, with his head in his hands, said to me, "That's it Vince – no more."

'Dennis Tueart was also terribly upset when he got sent off for headbutting a Hartlepool player in a cup-tie. Things got worse for Dennis when he found out it was an old schoolmate of his.

'But to finish on a happy note, in those Piccadilly days we would broadcast live from and to the ground, giving team news, traffic reports and the like, from about 1.30 p.m. through until kick-off. One day I was sitting at the back of the main stand with my checked overcoat and earphones on and it was about 1.45 p.m., the time when there are only a handful of people about.

'Anyway, this guy walked towards me wearing the full army battledress, top to bottom, helmet and all. He looked like he was ready to invade Vietnam. After speaking to the producer, it was agreed that we should put this guy out live on air.

'At about 2.10 p.m. I gave him the big introduction. I think the guy's name was something like Paul Johnson from Burnage. I said, "Well Paul, obviously a proud soldier, dressed ready for action. Tell me, just what do you do in the army?" He said, "I'm a cook!" God, did I feel a pillock – I got some terrible stick for weeks after that!'

JOHN STAPLETON

JOHN STAPLETON, former presenter of BBC Television's *Nationwide* and nowadays *The Time, The Place*.

'I have to say I am now an exiled Blue, living as I have for the last 25 years or so in London. Working on *The Time, The Place* means I spend three or four nights a week away from home and is one of the reasons why I have not been to Maine Road for about 15 years. My support has been given at places like Chelsea, Arsenal and Tottenham. Next year, unfortunately, it will be at Charlton, Reading and Southend – just for the one season, though.

'Having been born in Boundary Park Hospital I also admit to having a soft spot for Oldham Athletic, but ours has always been a Manchester City family. Both my father and grandfather followed City, and my grandfather Harry actually attended the first-ever game at Maine Road back in 1923.

'My first seven years were spent in Saddleworth and as we didn't have a car, I have fond memories of the two bus/one trolleybus trips to Maine Road for home games. I can remember watching Stanley Matthews's Blackpool from the now seemingly precarious position of the tunnel wall in the Kippax corner, and have lost count of the number of times I was passed over the heads of adults to a safer and more advantageous position.

'Like Joe Corrigan, I too remember the 1981 FA Cup final. For me, they have to be the best and worst games I have ever been to. I watched the games with fellow BBC presenter Michael Wood and I will never forget the agony of poor Tommy Hutchison. To this day I still cannot fully comprehend what he must have gone through. One outstanding recollection for me was Steve MacKenzie's superb volley in the replay. Then, of course, the Argentinians came into it and unfortunately the game was lost.

'My wife Lynn videotaped the games for me and I have depressed myself many times since, pondering on the fact that we were so close. My son Nicholas, who is eight, is the fourth generation Stapleton to follow the fortunes of City. Unlike other schoolboys of the same age, he will not be swayed by more successful sides, knowing that being a City fan is a lifelong sentence.

'A further irony occurred less than 12 months after that cup final. I was covering the El Salvador elections for *Newsnight* when the Falklands War broke out and I was sent to Buenos Aires as a "behind-the-lines" correspondent. It seemed as if I couldn't avoid the Argentinians during the early 1980s!'

IAN PENNEY

And what of the author, the man who has spent upwards of 20 minutes putting together this classic of world literature? As the 'blurb' on the jacket says, I have been following the fortunes of Manchester City since 1966. During this time I have seen who knows how many games – some, it has to be said, a lot more memorable than others. Take for instance the famous 'Ballet on Ice' against Tottenham back in 1967. The bus was late and when I finally got in the Blues were a goal down. Nice of them to wait until I got there before they started playing. (City won the game 4–1.)

Also the 5–1 victory against FC Schalke 04 in the European Cup Winner's Cup, one of the many tremendous midweek European games. Like Gary James I too could remember the overweight and unfit Rodney Marsh making his debut in 1972, and like Ian Brightwell, who could ever forget that magnificent triumph over United?

On the other hand I have also witnessed disappointments, not least against Wolves at Wembley in 1974 and against Liverpool in the last game of the 1995–96 season when just one more goal would have secured our place in the Premiership.

The most bizarre game I have witnessed in all these 30 years, though, took place in 1978. It was a UEFA Cup tie away against AC Milan. As one of a party of four, I flew early on the Wednesday morning for the game which was due to kick off at eight that evening.

After being overtaken by Concorde it was bright sunshine that greeted us at Milan airport. We were taken to our hotel where we changed and then made our way to one of the many roadside bars. It was here that we grasped the language fluently and in remarkable time: 'Quattro beero, please'. Pretty good, eh?

At about four o'clock one of the locals entered the bar and approached us. 'You boys over for game?' he asked. 'Yes,' we replied in unison. 'Game off,' he says. 'Off, what are you talking about?' He went on: 'Fog. Fog come down from mountains. Game off.' Quick as a flash we all rushed to the nearest window. The sun was still shining brightly and we could literally see for miles. 'Oh yes, very funny,' we said. The local was still adamant: 'No, no is off – fog!'

About 6.30 p.m. the coach arrived to take us to the ground. Within an hour the aforementioned fog had made its appearance. We were dropped off about 30 yards from the ground and we couldn't see a single brick of the massive San Siro walls. We eventually made our way in and all we could see were hazy images of the many fires started on the terracing to keep the Milan fans warm. Any hint of green grass was completely out of the question.

There were many announcements over a high quality public address system; the only thing was not one of them was in English. After what seemed an eternity – it was probably 90 minutes or so – we were finally told that there was no chance of play that night. We were then told to go to the ticket office where we could get replacement tickets for the rearranged fixture tomorrow, kick-off 12 noon.

Because our return flight was at two o'clock this put us in a tricky position. We could either miss the second half or miss our flight. At half-time the Blues were leading 2–0. (For our younger readers, this is not a lie, honestly.) We decided the game was ours and it was safe to get the flight back.

The coach back to the airport was driven by a Milan supporter who had a television over his rear view mirror and spent the entire trip watching the second-half. Great, we thought, we won't miss anything. We nearly missed everything when Milan pulled a goal back. The driver leapt from his seat and began jumping around in the aisle. Cries of 'Would you kindly sit down please' (or similar) came from every seat on the coach. Just before we boarded the plane, Milan equalised and the leg finished 2–2. Two weeks later Milan came to Maine Road and were soundly beaten 3–0 in the return leg. Their interest in Europe, for that season at least, was over.

Only City fans could travel all the way to Italy for 45 minutes of football!